D1452909

THE TABLE

What are you leaving on "The Table"?

DR. PATRICK IVEY

GUEST AUTHORS: DR. STARLA IVEY, AKEEM ROBINSON, AND DEREK LEGE

Print ISBN: 978-1-54399-751-4

eBook ISBN: 978-1-54399-752-1

"If you don't know the game, you're going to get played!"

—Barry Nembhard, Entrepreneur

DEDICATION

To my wife, Starla, and my daughters, Paisli and Serena, for supporting me and sharing me with many other people. We have all sacrificed to help others, and I couldn't have done what I love doing without your love.

To all my former teammates, who I call my brothers. We grew together through adversity, challenges, victories, losses, and championships. We formed a bond through blood, sweat, and tears that kept us close many years later.

To all the former student athletes I coached for over twenty years. I learned more from you than I ever taught you. You were the fuel to my fire, and I appreciate you allowing me to grow through your dreams and efforts.

CONTENTS

FOREWORD

I filtered a long list of different educational institutions down to five and had the printed applications on my desk. I had imagined the furnished studio apartment in all of the big cities, and I had already planned wardrobe selections for my first days of work based upon the season and region.

I looked up to my office door to see a familiar face adorned with an unfamiliar facial expression. "Coach" Pat Ivey had something on his mind, and I would later find out, on his heart. Fresh off of another graduation from the University of Missouri with a Masters of Education in Gifted Education, I was ready to hit the job market and start my professional career. The anxious excitement and internal elation from (finally) completing this process had taken over my day to day for weeks, but Coach was not in the mood to celebrate with me today. I was fully expecting Coach to congratulate, edify, encourage, and stimulate critical thinking of my next steps toward becoming a professional educator. Little did I know, he filled the doorway, my office, and my mind-set with a different sentiment.

Coach asked me, "What's next?" I replied, "What do you mean? I'm done! I graduated and I'm about to move! I am ready to make some real money!"

Coach responds with, "NO, what's *next*?" I was puzzled and was not following his prompt. He continued, "P-H-D. DOCTOR EK." I smiled and shrugged it off. I was not in the mind-set to think about more school, more check-to-check life as a graduate assistant, or completing the 'big bad wolf' dissertation. No one that I knew, other than really smart people, go on to achieve PhD status. I was definitely not one among those…

Coach said "Doctor Ek," smiled as he watched me absorb the thought, and then reversed out of my office door not saying another word. After multiple follow-up conversations and deliberations with Coach, and others, I decided that I would take the leap of faith, the courageous chance to succeed, and the life-changing steps to secure a terminal degree.

Inherently at play here were the common fundamentals that I had learned from Coach through the previous five years of interactions: hard work and attention to detail; competition and fractional advantage; goal setting and goal achieving; delayed gratification through process and program; and resilience, innovation, teamwork, and intrinsic motivation.

If and when you are placed in the position to accept a challenge to holistically improve yourself, my lived experience continues to prove that seizing the opportunity works out for your good 100% of the time. Do not be confused, though. The situation does not always work out the way(s) you initially imagined, but you always reap internal and external rewards along the complex journey. That is normal—let it become your new normal.

Where I am from, leaving anything on the table is not an option. Basic survival demands that you regularly operate in an exhaustively resourceful manner. I continue to be blessed by the guidance of Dr. Pat "Coach" Ivey as he demands this level of intentional tenacity and high performance from me in my adult life. Coach's "Oracle-like" vision impacts many of my daily thoughts, words, and actions.

Dr. Bradley Ekwerekwu

Former College and Professional (NFL) Athlete

PREFACE

I have heard a lot of people talk about what sports taught them. A mentor of mine, Dr. Rick McGuire, told me that athletes learn from coaches. This book is a resource for student athletes in high school or college as well as professional athletes. The purpose of this book is to inspire all athletes to take full advantage of their opportunities as an athlete. What are you leaving on the table? This is a metaphor for the opportunities we all have when we have a seat at the table of sports or any situation for that matter.

Give instruction to a wise man, and he will be still wiser; teach a righteous man, and he will increase in learning.

—Proverbs 9:9

INTRODUCTION

Have you ever said to yourself, "I wish I knew back then what I know now?" Growing up I was always interested in learning and gaining knowledge. As I grew older I learned it was much more important to be able to apply that knowledge. For me, looking back and reflecting has always been a part of my learning process. To me, it was a way to not just avoid repeating mistakes but also learn how to improve. I've also been very competitive, so having information and learning from that information always seemed to fit with my quest to be the best that I could be.

I grew up in Detroit, Michigan, where it was all about the survival of the fittest and where violence and distraction were becoming the everyday norm. Despite the external environment, my parents did a great job, and I also had good teachers, which gave me an advantage in the classroom. I always wanted to be the best that I could be in the classroom and be a good student. I enjoyed being in class as this was usually a safe place to be. I was always encouraged and challenged to improve and be better. I believed I could become whatever I wanted because of the strong foundation I was provided. Looking back, I was privileged to have really good parents and teachers.

I enjoyed most of my experiences while going to elementary school but middle school was a slightly different story. Academically, I continued to have good experiences, but the environment in the hallways, bathrooms, and outside of school began to change for the worse. It seemed like from the first day of entering the middle school there were fights, drugs, and guns. It was well known that on Fridays if you wanted to be safe, you should run home as soon as school ended. There were many Fridays or other days when I ran home just to avoid the fighting or gunshots, although, there were some days I couldn't outrun the violence and fights. Sometimes there was more than one person to fight and there was even one instance where I was threatened to be shot and killed.

Due to the nature of this environment, I was forced to think about safety and protection in ways that someone so young shouldn't have to. When I was ten years old, my mother decided she would take me to the football field as a way to further my development. In other words, I needed to get tougher. I would play for the Eastside Dallas Cowboys, a part of the Police Athletic League (PAL). My first coach was Coach Brock who was the best person I could have ever hoped for, as it was my first time playing football. Coach Brock was tough, loving, caring, and always consistent. He lived in the projects and rode his bike to and from practice. My first year playing football we went undefeated and not one opponent scored a point.

Coach Ogletree, or Coach "Tree" as we called him, was the next coach I would play for on the B team. We went undefeated as well. Coach Tree was very similar to Coach Brock except he was more patient and allowed us to make a few more mistakes. I now see this as a good thing because we were older, and it was important for us to try new things. Both Coach Brock and Coach Tree were instrumental in my development because I learned a lot about myself—they helped me define who I wanted to be.

Both Coach Brock and Coach Tree prepared me for high school football. I played football in high school at Cass Technical High School under Coach Rowland. Coach Rowland was a blend of both my parents, with the patience of my Dad and the discipline of my Mom. Coach Rowland allowed the team leadership to develop in ways that not many other coaches would. He let the leadership develop through autonomy where he gave us the ability to make choices.

Coach Rowland's leadership style was very useful as we were maturing into young men. For example, I was allowed to completely make my decision about which college I would attend. My parents and my coaches were very similar in this regard. I was fortunate enough to have academic and athletic choices. As a matter of fact, I even had an Evans Scholarship for being a golf caddie. As I look back, these choices were available to me because of making many other good choices.

I talk about "CHOICES" in this book as the first theme. Another word for choice is autonomy—the ability for one to make choices for oneself and by oneself. Having been a College Strength and Conditioning Coach I learned the importance of autonomy when trying to develop self-determined and self-motivated athletes. The ultimate goal of coaching is getting athletes to apply what is being taught. If a coach can foster an environment that allows athletes to make choices, it creates a team full of self-starters. This is important because athletes will spend more time away from coaches and with their teammates and friends.

The second theme in this book is "CHARACTER DEVELOPMENT." The chapter on Personal Development was written by Coach Akeem Robinson. Coach Robinson is currently a Director of Athletic Performance at Southeastern University in Lakeland, Florida. Personal development is about the steps one takes to become a mature person. It's about knowing your identity because you've made many choices to develop it. I follow up Coach Robinson's chapter on Personal Development with a chapter on Leadership Development where I highlight being put in a position or an environment that allows the traits of a leader to be taught, encouraged, and affirmed.

The final chapter under the theme of Character Development is relationships. When I was playing football in high school, college, and professionally, I didn't understand the power of relationships. I didn't understand the power of the relationships I had with my teammates, coaches, administrators, professors, alumni, boosters, politicians, public servants, etc. I rarely had a meaningful conversation outside of talking about football and sports with many of the people who were really close to the program. Seldom was it a conversation about faith, finances, family, money, building wealth, life after sports, or what career path I would choose. As I look back, I didn't know about the power of leveraging those relationships to help me later in life.

The third theme in this book discusses "MONEY AND WEALTH." This topic is very important today in athletics, whether high school, college, or professional. There are many sobering statistics (i.e., bankruptcy) as to what happens to the majority of professional athletes the years after they are done playing. I believe with the right information, awareness, and resources, many of these negative statistics could be diminished, reversed, or altogether avoided. In this book I am discussing the importance of making the right choices fostered through character development. I believe if athletes have the right information and the ability to make the right choices, it will lead to better decision-making regarding their money, which can positively impact their wealth.

For the Money and Wealth theme, the two chapters are written by Dr. Starla Ivey and Derek Lege. Dr. Starla Ivey is a college professor and teaches personal finance. Derek Lege is a College Athletic Performance Coach who also invests in the stock market. There is a strong need to do more financial education with students in general. Our purpose of discussing money and wealth is to help educate athletes, and those who work with athletes, so we all can benefit and start to get different results.

The final theme is "LIVING LIFE." In my opinion, sport and coaches provide a great opportunity to teach young people and prepare them for life. The three chapters under the theme Living Life are entitled "Life after Sports," "Focus and Family," and "Pass the Baton to Teach Others." We all know that one day being a high school, college, or professional athlete will end. We also know we need to do a better job of preparing athletes for that day. I emphasize the importance of "Focus" because focus is all about choices and skills. I can't think of anything in my life that is more important than being focused on what is important to me. There are many aspects of life, but none more important than my family. My family is very important to me. In fact, it was the same for most of the coaches and athletes I have coached or played with. Most athletes will say when asked, "What is your why?" their response is "my family." The final chapter is titled "Pass the Baton to Teach Others." I believe in order for our society to continue developing we must teach the young what we know and prepare them for a life worth living.

The ability for us to reach our goals in life depends on the choices we make now and in the future. The gift of choice is one of the greatest gifts we've been given. These choices we make help form our character. In life, we are constantly choosing and developing our character. Understanding who we are and our purpose in life can help us choose what we want to do. There's a lot of power and understanding with economics, a lot to gain with knowing how money works and how to build wealth. If we want to be the influencers who help make our society a better place to live, we must understand how to manage our finances.

Over the years, I've learned what matters most in my life—my faith, my family, and my friends. One day, you won't be able to play sports like you did when you were in high school, college, or in the pros. I can tell you from personal experience, there is life after playing sports! But, while you're still playing make sure you have a plan, or at least start developing one. Make sure that while you are an athlete, you are still growing outside of the sport. Make sure you're learning something every day that you can use now and later in life.

CHOICES

"Never go one day without learning something!"

—Al Ivey

It's important to understand the gift of choice is one of the greatest gifts in life. The choices we make have both direct and indirect impacts on our lives and those around us. Choices are basically just thoughts we have that lead to an action, which inevitably has a consequence. The consequences for our choices and actions can be positive, negative, immediate, delayed, etc. The choices we make are important!

When I was a college football player at the University of Missouri, I attended chapel service during the football season where sometimes we would have guest Chaplains deliver the message. I remember one of the best and most important messages I ever heard was a discussion focused around the most important choices you'll ever make.

I remember each one of the words started with the letter "M." The first word was "Master" followed by the question, "Who will you serve?" Will it be material things, or will it be faith based? The second "M" word was "Mission," described as your "Why" and "What." It's important to discover your purpose in life so you can work to accomplish it. The third "M" word was "Marry" followed by the question of, "Who will you marry?" The Chaplain said this decision was paramount, as this would be the person you would choose to spend the rest of your life with. The fourth "M" word was "Money" where he spoke about having the right perspective on money. Money is important because it's necessary to support your family and to execute your mission. Having the wrong motivations around money can lead to a life filled with negative consequences. The fifth and final "M" word was "Multiply" with the message/question of, "How will you use your mission and money to help others?" It's important to gain knowledge, skills, and experience to help and teach others. Others may be your spouse, children, family members, friends, or anyone. He taught us how all these "M" words could impact our lives and everyone around us. To this day, I've never forgotten that important life lesson.

CHOOSING YOUR IDENTITY

I've met and coached a lot of athletes who placed their identities in the sport they played. There are pros and cons to choosing to do that, no pun intended. One of the pros of placing your identity in sport is that it can drive you to greatness by being a strong source of motivation. I've been around athletes who ate, slept, and breathed their sport, all day long. Some were the best at their position or sport, and a few of them excelled far enough to be professional athletes in the sport they loved. But, as Neil McCauley says in my favorite movie, *Heat*, "there's a flipside to that coin." On the other side of that coin is the person who you are left to be when you are voluntarily or involuntarily no longer able to play that sport.

There's the "dark side" of having placed your total identity in sport. I've seen the cons of placing your total identity in sport. On the dark side of the coin can be depression and loneliness. It's important to know and remember that playing your sport is what you do, and not who you are!

I also had teammates who thought they were entertainers or musicians more than they were a football player. That's like living in a false reality within a false reality. That doesn't make any sense! Today when I meet with athletes, I want to know what their "why" is and what they want to do after they're done playing football. Then I ask them, "How are you going to do it?" This helps them to begin thinking about who they're choosing to be, as opposed to being what they do. Not every athlete is going to be a professional athlete, but every athlete is going to be a professional at something, hopefully.

It's important to know what your purpose is in life. It's important to place your value into areas like your faith, family, people, and relationships. As a student athlete, I tried to balance what I believed and what society was telling me to believe. As a student athlete, I had not truly looked inside of myself to know or identify what my "why" was.

It seemed like the longer I played football, the more of my identity became wrapped up in being a professional athlete. The more time I spent perfecting my craft, the more I gave up who I was without football to become the total football player. And, to a certain extent at that level, you're almost required to do so. I think the one thing that helped me to avoid the identity crisis some of my teammates had, is I had a plan to direct my passion into becoming a coach. Coaching allowed me to be around sport and athletes.

One of the best lessons I learned in life is to not place too much value on material things, they come and go and can be taken away. It's not easy to stay away from the message society teaches us. Sometimes that message takes the form of, "The more you have the happier you'll be." Other times the message becomes, "What you have is not enough or good enough." And still at other times the message is, "If you have more than someone else you are better." I think one of the most damaging messages is if you don't have anything then you are worth nothing. I think one of the most dangerous conflicts we have is trying to accumulate more than someone else and placing our identities in the things we have rather than who we are.

"If you can close your eyes and visualize it,
you can open your eyes and realize it!"

—Keyon Dooling

If you can know what your "why" or purpose in life is then you can operate with a passion that never decreases. Knowing your "why" creates strong internal and intrinsic motivation. It's important to be motivated from within because you don't have to depend on someone else or something else for your drive and determination. When the fire comes from within, you don't need someone else's words or for someone else to be there for you to bring your best. People love being around someone who has fire and passion about who they are and what they are doing. The best students are the ones who are driven from within to learn the knowledge. The best athletes are the ones that are driven from within to be the best that they can be and always perfecting their craft. The best employees are the ones that are passionate about their purpose in life and how they want to contribute to society.

Admittedly, it wasn't until I was a coach that I truly identified what my "why" was. I can remember when it all started coming together for me. It was around 2003 when I was the Director of Strength and Conditioning at the University of Tulsa and the Head Coach was Steve Kragthorpe. Coach Kragthorpe led a voluntary program where we dove into a book written by Rick Warren titled, *The Purpose Driven Life*. This book helped me identify my why, and this is where I discovered I wanted to help people maximize their human potential. The professional career in which I chose to do this was being a Strength and Conditioning Coach and the weight room would be my classroom. For over twenty years, I dedicated my life to being a coach. It was also during that time when my identity became more about being a good husband and father. Once I became a father, I became a better person and a better coach. I learned to better understand love, kindness, servanthood, and patience in the process.

As a coach, I spent a lot of time helping my athletes develop their identities, inside and outside of their sport. One of the best examples I can remember, is a former football player named Kip Edwards. Kip always took the information we were sharing as coaches and he applied it. One day he told me that he had taken a personality assessment in one of his classes. He believed the information he learned about himself helped him to be a better person and leader because he knew himself better. Personality assessments can be a very useful and powerful tool. If you know what your strengths are you can lean on those strengths. Kip believed that if everyone on the team knew what their strengths were, they could be confident in who they were because they would know themselves better. He believed if you had a team full of players who could rely on their strengths, they could better assimilate as a cohesive unit. So, we had a professional group from campus come and do an assessment to determine each player's personality and strengths. After the results were compiled, we decided we would have each class of players receive their information as a group. We divided the team by their natural freshman, sophomore, junior, and senior classes. This became a powerful moment because each player collectively knew what his and his teammates' strengths were, by academic class. The senior class took this information very seriously, as they knew they had to apply the information immediately for that team to be as successful as it could be. Kip taught us the better each player knows himself and what his or her identity is, the better they can contribute to the overall success of the team. Kip Edwards has since graduated and is on a career path to become a great head coach one day.

There are some very sobering statistics about the percentage of athletes that make it to the professional level in their sport. Reports I've seen say that 1% to 2% of collegiate athletes make it to the professional ranks. I often talk with athletes who know the statistics, yet the percentage of hands that gets raised in a room when you ask the question, "How many of you are going pro?" is still around 50% to 75%. The average career in the NFL or most professional sports is around 3.5 to 5.5 years. The question I ask athletes is, "What are you going to do when you're done playing your sport?" I asked them to do the math on how old they will be. Most of the time that age range is around 25 to 27 years old. The next question is, "What are you going do for the next 30 or 40 years before retirement age?" Asking this question helps athletes to think about how they form their identities, and who they are at that current point in time.

The pain of regret is strong and is something most people would choose not to have. As a student athlete, ask yourself the question, "Am I putting in the necessary work to have the opportunities I want?" You don't want to look back at the end of your life and say, "I didn't give it my all." The "woulda, coulda, shoulda" will eat you alive. Make sure you are surrounding yourself with positive people. You want to be around the kind of people who are challenging you and encouraging you to be the best version of you every day. You want to be around people that are helping you to understand your opportunities. If you're in high school, listen to your coaches, teachers, and counselors who are trying to help and show you the path to success. When they look back, student athletes always comment on how fast the time went. You need to leverage every opportunity you have to get to the next level. Whatever that next level is, you must begin thinking that way!

Being a positive person requires you to think positively. The importance of positive self-talk is often underestimated. You are your thoughts, and your thoughts are your own conversation with yourself. Most of the conversations people have with themselves are negative so you have to change this within yourself. Whenever you are thinking a negative thought, all you have to do is turn that negative thought into a positive thought. You can only think one thought at a time, so you should make the thoughts you have positive thoughts. The conversations you have with yourself are some of the most important conversations you will have. So, that being the case, you should aim to make those conversations positive conversations. You have to work on this all the time, every day. There are many messages you have to filter throughout the day to make sure that you stay in a positive state of mind. If you want positive actions, you have to have positive thoughts. If you want positive results, you have to have positive thoughts. If you want to achieve your dreams in life and be successful, you have to visualize yourself being that person.

If you listen to some of the most successful athletes, you'll notice them talking about the importance of visualization. Visualization is seeing your thoughts happen before they actually happen. You'll hear some of the most successful athletes talk about how they visualize themselves being in a high-pressure situation and being successful in that situation. Because they visualize themselves being successful in different situations, when they're confronted with that moment they feel like they've been there before. The most successful athletes can give very vivid descriptions of the moments when they want to have success. Visualization is a good way to train yourself into believing that you have been in that situation before and you've had success in that situation.

It's necessary to visualize yourself not only in successful situations but also when you don't have the success that you wanted to have, and how you will react. I'm not asking you to visualize yourself losing, but rather visualize yourself reacting to a situation that might be outside of your control. Here is a saying I share with athletes to help them to be more mentally and emotionally ready and stable for life's curveballs.

Be prepared in advance to have the greatest day of your life, while you're prepared in advance to possibly receive some of the worst news you have ever heard.

What this means is you should visualize yourself having all kinds of successes in advance of them actually happening, while you are simultaneously prepared to possibly experience adversity. While I was coaching, there were several times when athletes would tell me they used this quote to help them get through a tough situation or period in their lives. One particular athlete I remember was the starting quarterback of a team I was coaching. He lost his grandfather, who was the patriarch of his family, just before the start of the football season. While he was having success on the field, he was dealing with a very difficult situation off the field. He was prepared in advance to have great success while he was prepared in advance to receive some awful news. Through his mental and emotional preparation, he was able to be a great role model for his teammates and his family.

CHOOSING A PATH

Who is helping guide you while you are an athlete in high school or college? Who is showing you what the opportunities are? Who are your mentors? Many athletes end up feeling like they blinked twice and their tenure in sports was over. You have to be prepared in advance for the next thing. You should start thinking this way if you have not already done so. As Dr. Stephen Covey says, you must begin with the end in mind.

Knowing who you are and your purpose in life is helpful in so many ways. When you know who you are and what you believe, in my experience, the clearer your vision will be with what you want to do. Some high school and college student athletes don't know what they want to do after they're done playing their sport. Some student athletes know exactly what they want to do after they are done playing sports.

Sports where being a professional athlete is more glorified causes some student athletes to more easily fall into the trap of only seeing themselves as a professional athlete. It takes a lot of time and preparation to be a professional athlete. Trust me, I totally understand, and I get it. However, if you fail to plan then you are planning to fail. I've heard many reasons for why some student athletes don't think about what they want to do after they are done playing their sport. The reasons span from the lack of role models, counselors, teachers, or coaches who care, to time, etc. As an athlete, you have to assume the responsibility for your own direction. Don't let other people decide your future, don't let excuses get in the way of preparation. Knowing what you want to do after you are done playing is very important because if do, you will make better, more informed choices earlier.

Athletes who don't know what they want to do often don't take the right coursework. If you don't know what you want to do, you delay the decision to pick the right major and curriculum. I was once told by someone who worked in academic services that if you struggle your academic freshman year in college, it eliminates 50% to 75% of the majors you can choose in college. If the classes you are taking are not connected to your purpose and what you want to do later in life, it can have a negative effect on your motivation. I don't have any empirical evidence, as this is only from my conversations and observations. Being motivated to go to class and to be present in class is very important. Being motivated to actually learn the content, because you know it applies to what you want to do later in life, is very important. Students who are unsure of who they are and what their purpose is in life have a harder time staying motivated to be the best student they can be.

When I went to college, I knew what I wanted to do but it was not connected to my purpose. I truly didn't understand or know what my identity was. I thought I wanted to be an engineer. But as I look back, I didn't want to be an engineer as much as I wanted to be a great football player and have a good social life. Academically, my second and third years were just as difficult as my freshman year in college. My grades were average and my motivation to go to class was very low, which severely limited my options. After my third year in college, I found myself on the edge of being academically ineligible. It wasn't until this point I started to search and develop who I was and what I thought my goals were. To remain academically eligible, I was directed to speak with advisors in the College of Agriculture at the University of Missouri. Located in the College of Agriculture, there was a major called Hotel and Restaurant Management. I remember after the first day I was enrolled in the classes, I shifted my goals. I told myself I wanted to be a professional athlete and own my own restaurant. I loved cooking, nutrition, management, and business classes, and the last two years of college were my best two years. I knew the coursework I was taking was connected to my goals in life and every day I went to class with a purpose. Nothing can beat being internally and intrinsically motivated to achieve something and accomplish your goals. As of today, I did achieve one of my two goals.

I made it as a professional athlete. But still today I think about the opportunity to own my own restaurant.

My "why" in life is to help people maximize their human potential. While I was a professional athlete, I had the opportunity to explore coaching. I found that coaching brought me just as much joy is being an athlete. I was finally able to connect who I was with my purpose and what I wanted to do professionally. The "how" was easy after I knew my "why." For me, it was a lengthy discovery process, which is not necessarily a bad thing. Actually, I think it is a very good thing. I think it is a good thing to be searching, developing, and growing every day.

I have found that student athletes who have been exposed to different professions have a better idea of what they want to do. There are many athletes whose role models are mainly athletes or entertainers. Role modeling happens to be one of the most powerful ways we learn. Whenever we can help athletes get exposed to professions outside of athletics, it can have a profound effect on their outlook. For example, once when I was coaching, we had a former player stop by the weight room to visit. He happened to be a president of a bank. I paused the workout session to allow him to address the team. Afterwards, one of the players came to me and said, "Coach, I never thought that a former college player could be a bank president." That student athlete later told me that moment shifted his focus and shaped his goals. I have heard of moments like this being called the gift of exposure.

As I mentioned, visualization is a very powerful tool. There is a quote, "if you see it you can be it." I have also heard the quote, "What the mind can conceive, and the heart can believe, the body can achieve." Just as important as it is to visualize yourself having success on the field, court, track, or in the pool, etc., it's important to visualize yourself having success as a professional in life. If you want, you can take a few minutes to try it out right now. Close your eyes and take a few deep breaths. Try saying some positive words, also known as positive affirmations. See yourself doing something you love. See yourself operating within your passion and having great success.

Let's take a few moments to talk about success. I like to look at success as not the destination, but the journey. I once heard a healthy way to look at success is asking yourself the question, "Are you currently doing what you need to be doing to get to where you want to be?" I would add to that, "Are you doing that while being the person you want to be?" I've asked many high school and college student athletes if they thought they were successful. Some of them would say no and, I would ask why not. They would say because they're not where they want to be. I would ask them, "Do you mean you don't want to be here in school taking classes and being a student athlete and trying to be the best you can be?" They will say, no, that's not what they meant. I would ask them, "Is what you're doing currently helping you to get to where you want to be?" And, they would answer in the affirmative. I would help them to see that success was not a destination, but it was the journey. You may not be playing as much as you want to play, or even be a starter on your team, but that doesn't mean you are not a success. If you are working hard every day to achieve your goals, then you are a success. You may not be making the salary you want or have the job you eventually want to have, but that doesn't mean you are not successful.

I once read a statistic stating 75% of college graduates go on to do something other than what they went to school for or majored in. I believe this happens for many reasons. Some students may change their minds during the course or maybe they never really knew what they wanted to do from the beginning. Maybe some of them learned new information and expanded their minds, which caused them to make different decisions about the path they wanted to take. Maybe some of them had a hard time finding a job in the field they wanted to work. And, maybe some of them started working in the field that they thought they wanted to pursue and found something else they were more passionate about. There may be many more reasons, but that should never stop anyone from pursuing their passion and understanding their "why."

To be successful in any chosen path, you have to be self-determined. You have to be driven from within, intrinsically. You will have to persevere, be resilient, and have grit. To be self-determined, you have to know your choices and then make the correct choices. You will need to have the right information and understand how important your relationships are with the people you need to connect with. A big portion of what you want to do in life will come from your source of motivation. Don't rely on others or material things for your motivation, but do just the opposite. Rely on self-motivation and reward yourself from within. Another stronger source of motivation is striving toward achieving something, rather than avoiding something. For example, when you are in class seek to learn and understand, rather than going to class to avoid getting in trouble. If you find yourself doing things to avoid something, ask yourself, "What is it that I want to get or achieve?"

Goal Setting

It is important to set goals. It's important to set all types of goals—short-term, mid-range, long-term, life, spiritual, academic, athletic, relationship, personal, professional, and many more. You always want to be striving for something. You always want to be setting new goals and accomplishing and resetting your goals. I also suggest writing down your goals where you can see them daily. You want to make sure you are S.M.A.R.T. with your goal setting. Here is what I mean by S.M.A.R.T.

- S – Specific

  Make sure your goals are specific. One of the best ways to know if your goals are specific is to make sure you know the smallest details of each step.

- M – Measurable

  You want to make sure you can measure your goals so you know when and how you accomplished them. Don't be afraid to break your goals down to one step at a time.

- A – Attainable

  You want to make sure you can attain your goals. I know this can be difficult to balance being optimistic and making your goals too easy. There is nothing wrong with making easy goals because you can always readjust and reset. However, if you find the goals you set aren't possible, you can adjust those also. You will learn over time what you can accomplish.

- R – Realistic

  Be sure your goals are realistic. Saying you want a 60 inch vertical jump is probably not realistic; maybe even graduating with a 4.0 GPA is not realistic. You can still achieve something great with the right preparation and execution. I am not asking you to not try to get a 60 vertical jump or a 4.0 GPA, I am saying don't measure success or failure with goals that may have been too far out of reach.

- T – Time-oriented

  You need to place a time limit on when you will achieve your specific goals. Meaning, you want to accomplish what by when. It's important to state, "I want to accomplish what by when." You may need to adjust the time as well. Sometimes you will accomplish certain goals quicker than you had anticipated and sometimes just the opposite.

The takeaway here is, "your goals are supposed to help you by providing guidance and motivation. You want to make sure your goals are specific, measurable, attainable, realistic, and time-oriented."

CHOOSING YOUR FRIENDS

Have you ever heard the phrase "birds of a feather flock together?" This means that people who have common interest or backgrounds tend to hang around each other. One of the most important choices and decisions is picking your friends. Who do you sit with in class and at lunch? Who do you spend time with outside of school and outside of your sport? Do the people you are spending time with have similar goals as you? If you want to be successful in life, you need to be around other people who want success as much as you do. Dr. Eric Thomas talks about wanting success as bad as you want to breathe. What he's talking about is do you want success as much as you want to live and stay alive. If you want success that much, then you have to choose good friends as much as you want to breathe. Don't allow people without goals, motivation, or a strong purpose in their lives to be around you or your friends. It only takes one bad apple to spoil the bunch, so remove the bad apples immediately.

Being a student athlete means you spend a lot of time around other people. You spend more time around your teammates and other students than you do around your own family. As I look back at my younger self, one thing I can say I did very well is I chose good people to be around. This ability to choose good people to be around and have good people around me has extended to my professional career as well. Making relationship decisions and choosing good people to be around is a skill. To be as successful as you can be, you will need to use this skill in all facets of your life. Good friends will give you good advice, especially in times when you are having challenging and emotional situations. The feedback you get from someone who has good character is invaluable. As I look back, some of my former teammates, especially the ones who knew what their purpose was, chose good paths and are very successful today. And on the contrary, those that did not understand who they were and what their purpose was, ended up choosing paths that were not as successful.

CAREER CHOICE AND EDUCATION

The question I often ask athletes is, "What do you want to do after you are done playing your sport?" Some know exactly what they want to do after sport. But in certain sports more than others, a greater percentage of the athletes believe they are going to be professional athletes in their sport. There's nothing wrong with having the highest goals possible as an athlete for your sport career. However, to reach the professional level, you need to have many goals on the way. Some will require the ultimate sacrifices but many will be accomplished on a daily basis. As I've mentioned before, the average professional career of a basketball or football player is somewhere between 3.5 to 5.5 years. There is a stigma surrounding life after professional sports and I want to help eliminate that stigma by helping athletes formulate a plan.

If you have not visualized or decided what you want to be doing professionally after your playing career is over, how can you choose what you want to study in college? How can you choose a degree at a university that will serve your needs? Which department has the degree program you would be most interested in because it relates directly to the work you want to do, professionally? Choosing the right degree program in college is not a simple or easy task, you have to do a lot of research.

In the first chapter, I talked about my motivations for why I chose the degree path to be an engineer. I liked many of the aspects of engineering, in particular, the math and science. Perhaps I would've been better served to have a purpose for being an engineer. If my motivations were to solve problems in the world to help society and humankind, maybe I would've been successful going down the path to be an engineer. Academically, I always worked hard enough and I had the background from attending Cass Technical High School. Attending a college preparatory high school and studying electrical engineering should have prepared me to continue to study that in college, right? However, after my freshman year in college, I realized my GPA wasn't high enough to be accepted into the engineering school. I made the mistake of putting all my time into studying for my engineering classes and I didn't know my other classes were just as important from a cumulative GPA standpoint. I didn't know enough to even ask the right questions. Don't repeat the same mistakes I did. Your cumulative GPA in your freshman year is vital to be accepted into the degree program, even after you have been accepted into college and are taking classes.

After not being eligible for the engineering program, I thought I may want to try a business school program. Once again, there was no connection with what I thought I wanted to do and what my purpose was. I spent the second and third years struggling in college because I was taking classes with very little connection to my purpose. In fact, I hadn't given much thought to what my "why" was! It seemed so hard just to go to classes because I wasn't very interested. I wasn't interested because I did not see how it connected to who I was and what I wanted to do. It wasn't until my fourth year in college that I started to enjoy classes. I went to the College of Agriculture to enroll in classes to remain athletically eligible.

In the College of Agriculture, Food and Natural Resources, I got a degree in Hotel and Restaurant Management. This degree program allowed me to learn things I was passionate about such as nutrition, preparing food, cooking and serving food, business principles, management, and other subjects. The College of Agriculture staff and faculty were always very helpful. What I found more important than any else is that they were excited about me being with them and wanted me to be successful. For some reason, having people in my corner for support has always been important to me. I've always wanted to be around people that wanted the best for me and I always wanted the best for the people I'm around. This transition was important because I remember this moment sparking a new dream. I still believe I will own my own restaurant one day, but for now, I'll keep using my nutrition and cooking skills for myself and those around me. It's important to have goals and dreams and to work toward those goals and dreams. I can still tell you everything I learned in class about nutrition and cooking food because I use it every day! I absolutely love it.

As another example, let me give you a hypothetical situation of someone who is studying something they are good at, but may not be passionate about. Let's say someone wants to be a writer, so they decide to become an English major, but their passion is really working with kids. If they want to connect their passion with what they've chosen to do professionally, maybe they should be a high school teacher or a college professor. What some people may do is decide to become a writer. Writing is a great profession for someone whose purpose is to enlighten the world with their words. But what about the person whose real passion is working with students and their purpose is to teach the young? Would they lose their way due to lack of connection and motivation? Could the writer supplement what they do professionally with something they are passionate about outside of their job? I've seen this work for some people and not so well for others.

As a coach, there were certain instances I was able to foresee when one of my former athletes could make a good coach. This was the same thing my strength and conditioning coaches in college saw in me. Dave Toub and Donnie Sommer told me what they saw in me while I was an athlete. Beforehand, I hadn't thought about coaching in college until they told me I should look into coaching. They saw what I had been searching for all along. They recognized where my passions were and believed I would make a good college strength and conditioning coach. Well they were right! I have always loved being around coaches and athletes, especially in the weight room. I ended up having over a twenty-year coaching career at the collegiate level. I helped many coaches and athletes find success along the way. Just like my coaches helped me, I always tried to help our athletes identify who they were, and what they wanted to do after sport.

Many student athletes believe their career choice will somehow come to them. They don't understand this choice is something they must be actively pursuing. Coaches don't give you positions; it's up to you to earn a position on the roster. Teachers don't give you grades, you earn your grades. Job and career choices are not given to you. You must go after them by actively pursuing what it is you want to do. First, you have to know yourself well and what makes you tick. What do you get excited about? What gets you fired up? What is something you get emotional about because you care so much? What keeps you up at night and gets you excited about waking up in the morning? Hopefully something! Hopefully, there is something that you can see yourself doing. I've heard over and over again that if you love what you were doing, you'll never work a day in your life. That saying means if you do what you love, it will not be something you dread doing. In fact, it would be something that if money wasn't an issue, you would do it for free. However, in life, we need to be able to provide financially, so having a job or career is important for most people.

Most student athletes can tell the successful athletes they like to emulate, or they see in themselves. They can tell you exactly why and what attributes those people have and why they admire them. They can tell you which characteristics are not as flattering as other characteristics in those people. They will know information about them such as where they are from, which school they attended, and what their statistics are. Most student athletes study successful athletes who do what they want to do from a performance standpoint. Many athletes watch hours and hours of video of their favorite athletes training and competing. Many coaches encourage their student athletes to study other successful athletes, especially those who perform at a high level. There is usually a huge video database of successful athletes at the disposal of current athletes. There are also many avenues online to search for your favorite successful athletes.

But many times, especially in athletics, the athlete part is overemphasized! Why do we focus on the athlete in student athlete so much? Often, the "STUDENT" athlete receives attention because it affects the student "ATHLETE." When student athletes are recruited from high school, often the recruiters use the success of former athletes who went on to play at the professional level as examples. In my experience, very few times will the student athletes who went on to be a professional in something other than being a professional athlete get used as highlights. In most cases, this information is not available. It doesn't get collected so most recruiters cannot tell recruits what the athletes who didn't go pro in their sport are doing. Maybe it's not collected because that's not what appeals to the masses of young people. In certain sports more than others, young recruits aren't thinking about connecting what they want to do after their playing career is over to the classes and what degree programs they should be seeking. Often there ends up being a huge academic disconnect between a prospective student athlete recruit and when that recruit becomes a student athlete in college.

In my experience as a coach, when athletes who haven't connected who they are to what they want to do show up on campus and that's when the battle begins. The battle of getting student athletes to go to class becomes one of the biggest problems to the sport coaches and the academic staff. Chasing athletes around now becomes an everyday routine to get them to go to class. Coaches and the academic staff have to make sure someone is checking classes every day. The coaches and the academic staff spend so many resources doing class checks. Classes must be checked before AND after class to make sure some student athletes arrive to class on time and don't leave early. Golf carts are purchased or rented to get staff around on campus to do the class checks. More staff are hired to make sure athletes are getting to class and staying in class for the full duration. Why do we continue to do it this way? Why don't we ask ourselves, "Why are some student athletes not interested in the information being taught in class?

I once had an interview to work in a collegiate athletics department for the position of Director of Strength and Conditioning. By the time I was done with my interview, the Athletics Director at offered me the position of Associate Athletic Director of Student Athlete Outcomes. This was unique and I had never heard of anything like this before. The Athletic Director wanted to track their former student athlete's success after college by determining if they were able to secure a job and if that job was in the career field they studied while in college. Most statistics stop at whether you graduated from college within a certain timeframe. This particular Athletics Director realized you have to begin with the end in mind. If you want athletes to be successful in life, and have the career they desire and deserve, you must make sure from the time they are recruited until they graduate from college that they're on the right path.

At another university, I had the chance to speak with the Head Coach of an Olympic sports team. I was amazed by his passion for his student athletes' outcomes. This particular Head Coach was super passionate about what his athletes were able to do upon graduation and if they were prepared for their careers.

This coach made sure the athletes on the team were able to secure internships and take the appropriate classes that would lead to what they wanted to do, professionally. After spending almost three decades around college athletics, I would say these two examples are rare and exceptional. Some degree programs require more time than others which may take you away from your sport. I've been around some coaches who discourage their athletes from being in certain degree programs that are more academically rigorous to protect practice time. I know this may seem far-fetched, but as an extreme example, I know of a head coach who encouraged the academic staff to steer their players into General Studies. Don't allow this to happen to you! Take control and make informed decisions.

I remember the day I shared I would no longer be in the engineering program with my position coach. He hugged me and congratulated me. He was happy because he said I would have more time to dedicate to football. I'll never forget that moment in his office and saying to myself, "wow, he doesn't care about me." I remember feeling at that moment the loss for any respect that I had for my position coach. This was especially disappointing because during recruiting I told him that I wanted to be an engineer and I needed support. Not only did I not receive the necessary academic support, but I was congratulated when I told him I would no longer be pursuing my dream to be an engineer. As I'm sitting here writing about this, I find myself still disappointed. I have no tolerance or respect for coaches who don't attempt to develop the athlete as a whole person. As an athlete, make sure you're getting the most from your coaches. If you're in high school and being recruited, make sure you are going to a university with a coaching staff that will care about you as a whole person. Make sure they can tell you about what their former athletes' successes are in life after sport.

Education and going to school is also about exploration. While you are pursuing your education, you should become more aware of different opportunities and career paths. This is a good thing. You may be discovering who you are and what your purpose is, which shapes what you want to do. The sooner you know what your purpose is and what you want to do, you can decide what career choice and be enrolled in the classes you need. This also allows you to work with counselors to get aligned for good internship possibilities. Internships are very important because this is where you can get real career experience. It's important to get real world experience before you graduate and you're really looking for a job.

You don't want to be the person who doesn't know what they want to do after they're done playing sports. Not knowing what you want to do career-wise makes it difficult to select an internship. There are still too many student athletes who graduate with a degree and minimal work experience in the field they want to pursue professionally. Some didn't take advantage of internships because they didn't have enough time or didn't take the time to do it. What I've seen all too often are athletes who have graduated with a college degree, yet don't have any idea what it is they want to do. This is a travesty. Too many athletes spend four or five years in college going to class, just receive a degree in something they have no desire to pursue. Please understand that you as a student athlete are also competing with students for jobs and careers.

If you don't have many examples in your life of someone who does something that you want to do, or does something very similar, you may want to visit a counselor at your school. They may be able to set you up with a Career Aptitude Test, or something that can guide you based on your preferences or personality. It's important to know yourself, as best as you can. There are different assessments and test available at your disposal. You just have to make sure you're actively pursuing this information and gaining knowledge about what is available. If you can select electives in high school or college, knowing what you want to do will help you with those decisions. Something we will talk about in a later chapter is the power of relationships. When you know who you are and what you want to do, you can begin connecting with those people in that arena and start to build relationships as early as possible. Many opportunities may arise from building a relationship with a person who is situated in the field you want to study.

CHARACTER DEVELOPMENT

"The true test of a man's character is what he does when no one is watching."

-John Wooden

Your character is the sum of your values, morals, ethics, principles, decision-making, and actions, just to name a few. To be the best version of you, you have to always be working and developing your character. It's not always easy to operate as a person of good character. It's not easy to always tell the truth and operate within that truth. It's not easy to always work hard and avoid being lazy. It's not easy to always treat people with respect when you have been disrespected. It's not easy to always take responsibility for your own actions and decisions. It's not easy to always try hard and do your best. However, developing your character is just like anything else, the more you work at it, the better you will get. If you are not the person you want to be yet, or if you are not the person who you say you are, that doesn't mean you can't work toward being that person.

The quote *character is who you are when no one else is looking* has a different meaning today than it did a few years ago. Social media and technology have greatly influenced today's society. Ten years ago this quote may have implied the question, are you the same person when no one is looking and in the presence of people? Now we are more accessible than ever. Also, today, you can be one person in the presence of people, another person when you're by yourself, and a totally different person on social media. On social media you can create an avatar to be whomever you choose. I think this can be very dangerous because to improve your character, you have to be constantly and actively working on who you are in reality. If we're spending more time on social media, and possibly creating an entirely different person, when do we get to actually work on the person we are?

As I look back, reading more may be the one thing I wish I had done differently. When I was in high school and college, I didn't enjoy reading very much. Most of the time I did everything in my power to avoid reading. Today, I know reading is about learning new ideas and gaining new experiences through someone else's words. Today, I love reading and one of my favorite books is *The Growth Mindset* by Dr. Carol Dweck. She talks about the difference between having a *growth* mind-set and a *fixed* mind-set. People who possess a growth mind-set believe they can learn anything if they just work hard enough, practice, and put in the right amount of effort. People with a fixed mind-set think they can't get better or increase their skill or knowledge in certain areas. The former are always working toward higher achievement and they believe they can always get smarter. This reminds me of one of my dad's favorite quotes, "don't ever let a day pass without learning something." I try using this same philosophy with myself and with my own children. I believe having a growth mind-set is fundamental to character development.

Reading scriptures can be another avenue to develop your character. There's a lot of wisdom written to help develop the spiritual side of your character. Two of my favorite scriptures are "Love your neighbor as you love yourself" (Matthew 22:39) and the golden rule, "In everything, do to others as you would have them do to you" (Matthew 7:12). The golden rule is a common ethic shared by most religions. Treating people with respect is an important characteristic to develop. To be the best leader you can be, you should try to find inspiration from as many areas as you can. As a leader, you may or may not be spiritual, but it is most likely some of the people you are leading will be spiritual. Plus, developing yourself holistically is not a negative. You may find you need to have faith in something, because challenging times will test your character and your intestinal fortitude. I encourage you to reach out to your spiritual community and get connected with exploring new ideas that will help shape and form who you are and who you want to be.

The next chapter is written by Coach Akeem Robinson, for a coach by a coach to best help athletes. I first met Coach Robinson at a football high school camp in St. Louis at De Smet Jesuit High School. He was the Head Strength and Conditioning Coach at the University of Missouri - Rolla, where he was volunteering at the camp we were hosting. I immediately took notice of Coach Robinson's energy and passion for people and athletes and we maintained close contact from that day forward. Coach Robinson would eventually join us at the University of Missouri as a Strength and Conditioning Intern. Prior to his arrival on our campus, he had been living periodically in his car. We were able to secure some living arrangements while he was interning with us where he was able to stay in a fraternity house and work as a house dad at night and intern for us during the day. This, among many others, is a reason why I chose Coach Akeem Robinson to write the chapter on personal development. I honestly cannot think of a person in whom I have witnessed more personal development than Coach Robinson. His passion to improve daily is infectious to all those around him, especially his athletes. Coach Robinson now serves as the Director of Strength and Conditioning at Southeastern University in Lakeland, Florida, which is close to his hometown Miami, Florida.

The chapter following personal development discusses leadership development. Developing leaders on and off the field is a passion of mine and I feel it is foundational to my life's purpose. I believe the success of a team or organization rises and falls on the leadership from the players/members on the team. Leadership fills the gap for many shortcomings. Team leadership will make sure that when things are going wrong, things get going in the right direction. The better and more leaders you have on a team, the better the team leadership. Team leadership also makes sure that when things are going right, they stay that way.

PERSONAL DEVELOPMENT
(BY AKEEM ROBINSON)

Student athletes are becoming bigger, faster, and stronger every day. They're competing at higher levels than we, as coaches, did when we played our sports. They are complex individuals with a variety of stresses on their plates including academics, sports, and life. In my experience, because student athletes are physically able to perform at an optimal level at eighteen years old, we assume they are prepared to function as adults in society as well. We tend to forget to develop the mind, emotional stability, and "real-life" knowledge of the student athlete.

For the student athlete to buy-in to the culture, demands, and expectations of the team, they have to feel supported physically, mentally, and emotionally. When coaches spend time developing the character of their student athletes, they directly increase the success of that player in competition while still preparing them for a life after sport. Coaching student athletes to reach their optimal potential, while still winning, is achieved by teaching, allowing autonomy, and creating intentional relationships.

Students always remember their favorite teacher, but they also remember the teacher they never learned from or always yelled at them. Coaches are teachers, mentors, and educators of sport and are tasked with the job to transfer their vast knowledge to their student athletes. Developing autonomous student athletes not only allows the coach to trust in their performance on competition day, but also instills quality routines, decision-making skills, and the ability to be contributing members of society after sport. Finally, creating intentional relationships between the student athlete and the coach increases the student athlete buy-in to the culture, goals, and expectations of the team. These quality relationships are crucial in helping players find their identity while still performing at their best. For coaches, intentional relationships increase dependability of the student athlete and trust in leadership within a team.

The job security of a coach is dependent on wins and losses. The financial stability of the coach's family relies on the consistency of winning records and renewed contracts. Because of this, as coaches, some have lost the fundamental principle of coaching—teaching the game, i.e., teaching the fundamentals, the purpose, and the why behind every decision, activity, and expectation given to the student athlete. Every kid remembers their best teacher and worst teacher because of an experience, conversation, or missed opportunity to learn. The same can be true for coaches. When coaches get caught up in developing players to win, they tend to lack transferring fundamental knowledge to be better moving forward when they are no longer a student athlete.

In my experience as a coach, after realizing the lack of awareness in student athletes regarding nutrition, mental awareness, and fundamentals for optimal performance, I've implemented a five- to ten-minute announcement portion into every training session. A former athlete approached me about making an impact as far as programming training sessions and preparing student athletes for optimal performance. I asked my current student athletes, "What are some of the principles we discuss during announcements, prior to our workouts?" Of the variety of responses, a few memorable ones included: "We check in mentally to see where we are, to make sure we understand that there is a bigger point in life," and "Our bodies are high-powered cars, so we need to make sure we treat them right." The former athlete was impressed by the knowledge of the players after just two weeks of training sessions.

The feedback I received justifies the five to ten minutes I spend teaching basic principles prior to their training sessions. I altered exercises or decreased sets and reps in order to provide this education time for student athletes. When you invest in the knowledge of your student athletes through your time, they are better prepared for being down by twenty points in a fourth quarter or behind by a few strokes in the pool. They can make it through five more events because they know how to prepare their bodies and their minds for competition. "Giving up" this time in a meeting, film session, or practice helps build a mentally equipped player, able to perform at their best, throughout an entire competition, season, and in their life moving forward.

When developing the character of a student athlete, teaching autonomy is a significant factor that is often lost, especially in team sports. Student athletes must develop their own voices, routines, and systems in order to perform at their best because they are the individuals competing, with the assistance of the coach. We want our student athletes to be self-sufficient and functional in society with or without a coach, teacher, or mentor in their life. Our job as coaches is to guide and direct these principles so the student athlete can carry them out on their own.

I've found that involving student athletes in decision-making can help reveal where the leadership is on a team, it can give a coach a different perspective that they are not able to see from a sideline, or it can give the student athlete a sense of ownership in the team. This adds to the "buy-in," as we previously discussed. I allow teams to begin warm-ups on their own, determine awareness training exercises, or discuss the tasks of the day based on how their bodies feel. These strategies gave me great results, not only during my training sessions, but I know these individuals will be better equipped moving forward when weighing factors in other life decisions.

How do we build autonomous student athletes? We put them in positions that force mistakes, critical thinking, or decision-making in order to develop strong problem solvers. Giving student athletes the platform to lead, develop, and teach others provides a sustainable foundation for further team mentorship. This foundation also allows student athletes to continue to grow as strong-minded individuals in their lives after competition.

As coaches, we've heard the saying "they don't care how much you know unless they know how much you care." Our student athletes don't care what we are teaching them until they understand the person teaching. Coaches spend numerous hours with their student athletes in meetings, during practice, and often at mandatory team functions. In season, this time is spent preparing for the next competition, discussing strategy, and working on becoming physically better student athletes. This causes us coaches to forget to check in and ask the simple question "How are you doing today?" and then really listen to the response. Reminding ourselves first, then our student athletes, that the sport is not their whole lives is incredibly important to developing player–coach relationships. The sport is not their identity; student athletes are still people contributing to society and should be treated as such.

A few years ago, I overhead some football players talking about a teammate who backed a car into a fence. I later approached this player to check-in and see how he was doing, asking if the story was true and if he needed anything. I learned that he never learned how to drive, thinking he would never need to learn. This five-minute conversation turned into a semester of Monday nights teaching him how to drive my truck around campus until he felt comfortable enough to pass the driver's test and buy his own car.

Coaches recruit good athletes. They recruit individuals that will perform well on competition day and contribute to the culture of the team. Developing these relationships doesn't have to take away from sport-teaching time, family time, or the rest of their lives. However, being a coach is a commitment to the student athlete that you will be there for them in support, guidance, and encouragement. This may look like meeting a player for coffee or lunch outside the office, asking how they are doing with classes prior to starting a meeting, or asking them for their opinion on a play, drill, or game strategy. Including student athletes and recognizing them as human beings with a life outside of the sport will increase the buy-in of the student athlete.

Teaching how to swing a baseball bat, block a volley-ball, or make a tackle is easy because you as a coach have likely done it before. Take the time to invest in the "real life" education of your student athletes by showing them the "why," asking them for opinions, and developing strong players in the game of life, not just during their years of eligibility. Allow your student athletes to explore, question, and create meaning behind the principles that you teach them within your winning culture. Giving them the tools to build their own foundations for their lives is just as important as helping them be the foundation for your team. Finally, the relationships you make with each student athlete should be with the intent of a lifetime friendship or mentorship. You are in a position of power but also of influence to make a difference to each of your players. Be intentional with the time, ask them how they are doing and in turn, they will care more about you as well. They will perform better and play better when they know their well-being is supported and valued. To care for something is easy but to show you care for someone is difficult. Use your coaching platform to show that you care.

LEADERSHIP DEVELOPMENT

Leadership must be developed and cultivated by the coaches and those who work very close with the team. Leaders are not born, leaders are trained and developed. There are certain personality traits some people are born with that may allow them to attract others more easily, but that is not leadership. There's also a difference between being a positive leader and a negative leader and I've had the opportunity to be around both. As a coach or a team leader, you have to get those who are very influential from a negative perspective to switch to be a positive influence. If you have coaches/teammates who are negative leaders, you have to get them to use their abilities to do positive things. If you are the person who is a negative leader, then you can change your attitude and actions. If you don't consider yourself a leader at all, change the way you think! Everyone has the capacity to lead in some area. Some people are more action-oriented and some are more vocally talented. To be the best leader you can be, you need to know yourself and what your strengths are. Don't try to be someone who you aren't because your teammates probably know if you are being authentic.

John C. Maxwell is one of my favorite authors who writes about leadership. One of my favorite books he wrote is *The Five Levels of Leadership*. Here are the five levels he writes about:

- Level 1: Position – Rights, people follow because they have to.

- Level 2: Permission – Relationships, people follow because want to.

- Level 3: Production – Results, people follow because of what you've done for the team.

- Level 4: People Development – Reproduction, people follow because of what you have done for them personally.

- Level 5: Pinnacle – Reputation, people follow because of who you are and what you represent.

As a Strength and Conditioning and Athletic Performance Coach, I always tried to develop as many level 4 and 5 leaders as possible. I found that when you invest in developing people as leaders, the whole organization's or team's performance rises. Level 4 and 5 leaders develop other leaders on the team, and they carry on the team message. For someone to be a level 4 or 5 leader, they have to go through the previous four stages of leadership. As a coach or captain on the team, you have to invest in people personally, by getting to know who they are and helping them to be as competent as they can be. It takes a lot of time and energy to develop leadership, but in the end it's always worth it.

One of the best leaders I ever had a chance to coach was Chase Daniel. Chase has played in the NFL for over a decade. He was an outstanding quarterback at the University of Missouri, a finalist for the Heisman Trophy award, and an All-American. While he was a good leader by action, what always stood out to me was his vocal leadership. Chase knew he had to guide others to reach their individual potential if they were to win Championships. Chase knew he had to help develop his teammates into Champions. One of the best examples I can remember where Chase used his vocal leadership was during a condition session. He asked for a quick pause to come out to speak with me just before we were about to finish the on-the-field training session with a conditioning segment. He told me the participation at the previous night's player run practice was not up to championship standards and the team needed some extra conditioning as a physical reminder of how important those sessions were. I conditioned the team until Chase and I felt the number of extra sprints made the point. As a leader, he would help to hold the team accountable to the championship standards the team established. He put himself in the position to be disliked by some of his teammates in order to hold everyone accountable to the dreams and goals they had as a team. I always look back on Chase Daniel as an example to what a real leader says and does. There were no boundaries with Chase using and developing his leadership skills. He would even use his skills with coaches! There are many more athlete examples I could use to demonstrate leadership, but Chase always stood out to me.

Some athletes I coached would ask me what I expected from them as a leader and how did I expect them to lead. I would always answer those athletes by saying it wasn't my job to tell them how to use their gifts, talents, and skills. Some athletes who were more introverted would sometimes feel uncomfortable being a vocal leader. They would tell me, "Coach, I'm not really the talkative type and I don't feel comfortable being a vocal leader, but you want us to be vocal leaders." My response would be, "to be a vocal reader, doesn't mean you have to stand up in front of the team and give great speeches." If you just talk to the person or your teammate standing next to you and give them guidance, advice, encouragement, positive feedback, etc., you're a vocal leader. In my opinion, it's never an excuse to not say what needs to be said. You may not want to deliver the message in front of the group or the team, but you can approach the individual. You can also relay what needs to be said to someone who is comfortable speaking in front of the team, and let them know what needs to be said.

John C. Maxwell is a critically acclaimed best-selling author who has written numerous best sellers on topics revolving around leadership. Another one of my favorite books written by him is *The 17 Indisputable Laws of Teamwork*. In the chapter titled, "The Law of the Big Picture," John writes "if you think you are the entire picture, you will never see the big picture." He believes the goal you have on a team is more important than the role. Everybody on a championship team doesn't get the publicity, but everyone can say they're a champion.

Some of my other favorite chapters in *The 17 Indisputable Laws of Teamwork* are "The Law of the Chain," "The Law of the Catalyst," "The Law of the Bad Apple," and "The Law of the Price Tag." "The Law of the Chain" speaks to a chain being only as strong as its weakest link. Using a chain as a metaphor is great because all the links are connected and each serves a purpose. If one or more of those links are weak, then that will become the breaking point within the chain. Within the team concept, the stronger links must strengthen the weaker links. This is where the team leaders are needed, because they must first identify the weak links, then form a strategy to strengthen them.

"The Law of the Catalyst" speaks to the players or people on a team who make things happen. They make the plays in the crucial times when the plays need to be made for the team to continue or generate its momentum. Championship teams have catalysts who step up when the pressure is high and deliver their best performances using their skills and talents. John C. Maxwell calls catalysts "get-it-done-and-then-some-people." They always get their job done first and then find other ways to make up for the team's weaknesses. Talent alone will not get a team to reach its full potential. Championship teams have a lot of players who know their roles and are accountable to delivering their best consistently.

The chapter titled "The Law of the Bad Apple" is one of the most important chapters in my opinion. In my experience as a coach, having bad apples on a team is the fastest way to cause its destruction and demise. To put it simply, a bad apple is a person with a bad attitude. Bad attitudes can destroy teams faster than good attitudes can put the team together. People who have bad attitudes are negative thinkers. Rotten attitudes ruin the team. My former head coach, Gary Pinkel, used to say, "You either have to change them or help them find a new home." Bad apples still have the ability to change their negative attitude and become a positive productive person and teammate.

"The Law of the Price Tag" speaks to the idea of there being a cost for success. On championship teams, everyone must be willing to pay the price to be a champion. Often the teams who don't reach their potential have players who aren't willing to pay the price. Here are four rules for the law of the price tag stated by John C. Maxwell.

- The price must be paid by everyone
- The price must be paid all the time
- The price increases if the team wants to improve, change, or keep winning
- The price never decreases

Ultimately, the law of the price tag is about sacrifice. Championship teams have leaders who are willing to sacrifice immediate gratification for the potential achievement of the big goal. As Coach Pinkel used to also say, "It's hard to win!"

This type of information would have allowed me to further develop my leadership outside of the team. As I look back on my college career as a student athlete, I wish I had been more involved with different social groups. I believe if I had more experience with how to conduct professional meetings, it would've helped me more, especially today as I'm a College Athletics Administrator. As a student athlete I don't remember being encouraged to participate in outside organizations or activities. Mostly, we were encouraged to spend most of our time thinking about our sport and doing whatever we needed to do to remain eligible to play our sport. Thankfully, that paradigm has evolved since then. Here are some other ideas and opportunities you may want to consider participating in to expand your growth as a leader.

Student Athlete Advisory Committee (SAAC)

This association-wide committee was adopted at the 1989 NCAA convention; it was formed primarily to review and offer student athlete input on NCAA activities, and propose legislation that affected student athlete welfare. There are usually two student athletes from each sports team who are designated to serve on the SAAC. Officers are usually voted on by the group.

This is a great way to be a part of a group that has a voice for the student athletes.

Leadership Council

Some coaches select a group of players on a team to be a part of the team's leadership council. Sometimes coaches select athletes they see leadership abilities in, and sometimes they select players who they predict will be good leaders in the future. One of the best examples I've seen of this is by the winningest Head Football Coach in Missouri football history, Coach Gary Pinkel. Coach Pinkel would select a few players from each class for a total of eleven to thirteen players. Coach Pinkel would spend time teaching leadership skills and use this group as a conduit for communication to and from the team. If there were any serious discipline issues, the leadership council would be involved and usually a strong determining factor for outcomes and decisions. If you can be a part of the leadership council, or recommend this concept to your coach, this would be great leadership development for you and your teammates.

There are opportunities for more social interaction in the spiritual realm with groups such Athletes in Action (AIA)/ Fellowship of Christian Athletes (FCA). These and similar organizations can also help you develop as a person and as a leader. Having a better understanding of who you are and what your beliefs are can help you as a leader. Drawing inspiration from different examples of people who have a strong sense of who they are through their spiritual faith can be powerful. Organizations such as AIA and FCA give athletes a chance to interact with other athletes who play different sports. This can be a strong support mechanism within the athletic community because you all have so many shared experiences. Many times, meeting athletes from other sports in a safe setting, such as AIA and FCA meetings, can provide much-needed support.

There are several committees and organizational opportunities on the college campus you can look into getting involved. Rarely do student athletes in college have a chance to get to know the other students on a deeper relational level. Most athletic facilities are separate from the academic campus, so having other opportunities can help you to get to know more people. Some of these people may become a part of your network after you're done playing your sport. You may also look for opportunities to get involved in student government or fraternities/sororities. These are also excellent opportunities to be around other leaders and develop your own leadership skills.

As coaches, we always want a team full of self-starters. Teams that have a lot of self-starters, or people who know how to get themselves going without much help from others are very motivated teams. Being a self-starter is a strong leadership quality. To be a leader you have to be motivated to get yourself going which also sets a great example to others on the team. When I went back to school to get my Doctorate in Sports Psychology, I learned about Deci and Ryan's theory of self-determination and intrinsic motivation. The self-determination theory requires three components—competence, autonomy, and relatedness. Coach Akeem Robinson also talked about the importance of autonomy in his chapter that covered personal development.

Competence means knowing what you're supposed to be doing and how to do it. Do you understand the techniques and fundamentals required to play your position? Competence is about knowing your alignment and your assignment and being where you're supposed to be at the correct time. It's also about knowing where your teammates are and what their assignments are. Competence is also about knowing and understanding the game plan.

Autonomy is the ability to make decisions and choices by yourself and for yourself or your teammates. It is important on championship teams for leaders to have the ability to make decisions and contribute to the team's direction. Having coaches who foster an environment that encourages this sort of freedom is important. Championship teams have leaders who can make decisions and contribute to the mission. Having coaches who foster an environment that encourages this sort of autonomous leadership is conducive to high performance which can lead to winning more games. There are many important decisions you face throughout the day and having the experience of making your own decisions and recognizing the consequences of those decisions directly translates to sport and life.

Relatedness is a term that describes how we as human beings are socially connected with each other. Being a part of the team is one of the strongest environments that provides many social interaction opportunities. Relationships with teammates and coaches can be very beneficial to accomplishing common goals. The next chapter will go more in depth discussing the value and power of relationships.

Ultimately, you have to take responsibility for your own leadership development. Don't wait for someone else to put you in position to be a leader. You should be constantly doing the work necessary to be ready, always be working on developing your character and your leadership. New roles can challenge you to improve your leadership and increase your leadership skills, but you need to be ready to learn. There are many ways to learn on your own, especially today with information at your fingertips through technology. Also, there are ways to learn and improve your leadership skills with very low cost. The resources available on-line are endless, and you should be able to search for whatever you need. There are many fantastic leadership books out there at your disposal. Find a topic you're interested in and dive into learning more about how that information can help you to be a more dynamic leader, and ultimately improve your character and the person you are.

RELATIONSHIPS

This may be the most important subject matter in this book. As I look back and I talk to my twenty-year-old self, I would say, "Make sure you spend most of your social time investing in positive relationships." I can look back and see when I was younger and where I took the time to invest in positive relationships and how it has continued to pay off today. The most important relationship I have with another person is with my mate. I met my wife in college, and we dated for several years before marrying. Fortunately, I was able to learn at an early age the importance of investing and spending time with positive people, especially the person you could end up with living with for the rest of your life. This is one the most important decisions ever I made. My suggestion to you is to make sure the person you are spending the most time with is someone who inspires and encourages you to be the best person you can be. Make sure the person who wants to be with you is also a person you want to help to be a better person.

Your Family

Your family constitutes the people who have supported you up until this point. No one's family situation is the same and should never be compared to someone else's. Some people come from two-parent homes where everything is intact and others come from situations more fragmented. Regardless of your situation, there are people around you who care about you and are trying to help you. When I pursued my Doctorate in Sport Psychology, through my dissertation writing I discovered something very profound as a major theme. The "Elite" athletes I have coached and researched who succeeded at the highest level all have something in common. They were all motivated to perform to bring honor to their family. Some of them told me directly they play for their last name and their purpose in life is their family. These elite athletes want to make people proud including their parents, siblings, children, and extended family. Through my research, I was looking to answer the question, "What did elite athletes do that allowed them to be more successful than most?" The answer was, "They play for their family and their last name."

Teammates

Some of the most powerful relationships you will have are the ones with your teammates. Some athletes on the team naturally think of their teammates as people who can help them accomplish their goals. Others think of their teammates as their extended family. In this book, we are answering the question, "What are you leaving on the table?" As a Strength and Conditioning Coach, one of my tasks was to help the players on the team get to know each other better on and off the field. I realized if each athlete knew themselves better, they could better present themselves to their teammates. This was counter to my own experience as a student athlete. My teammates and I weren't really encouraged to get to know each other beyond football.

If you're an athlete in high school or college, you'll probably spend the next four or five years being together with the players in your class. So now I want you to take a look at the rest of your life after you are done playing your sport and count the years. You and most of your teammates will go on to be very successful in life after sport, especially if you can realize the people you spend the most time with can help you later in life. With this kind of wisdom you'll be much further ahead. Make sure you get to know what your teammates want to do with their lives after sport. You will probably learn you have some common interests and you can partner up later in your professional careers. The relationships you can strengthen through the amount of time you spend with each other trying to achieve the same goal can be a great foundation for success later in life. As a coach, I would always encourage the athletes on the team to get to know each other better. I knew how important this was from my personal experience because at some point I realized I left many relationship opportunities on the table as a student athlete.

As of today, I've made attempts to reconnect with some of my old teammates and it's been very rewarding. For example, one of my teammates grew up in rural Missouri and is an avid hunter, whereas I grew up in the inner city of Detroit, Michigan, with few opportunities to go hunting. Approximately ten years after our college careers were over, I finally accepted an invitation from him to go hunting on his property and I loved it! I now try to go hunting as often as I can. The relationships I have forged over the past ten years because of developing a passion for hunting have helped me professionally and personally. I've even been able to pass this love for the outdoors and hunting to one of my daughters. This is just one example out of many that I could talk about.

Athletes from Other Teams

Finally, all of you should be of one mind. Sympathize with each other. Love each other as brothers and sisters. Be tender-hearted; and keep a humble attitude.

—1 Peter 3:8

Getting to know student athletes who play other sports are some of the best opportunities to capitalize on to develop relationships. If you are a multi-sport athlete, you already have this built-in network available. Just because the athletes on other teams don't play the same sport doesn't mean they can't relate to your challenges and experiences. The fixed-minded person cannot see past the false boundaries placed around the sport they play. Don't let these artificial boundaries stop you from developing relationships with people who have similar values and work ethic. Many of them want to be just as successful as you. The same values you learned from your coach and playing your sport are the same values everyone who is playing sports are exposed to. Getting to know other athletes on other teams is a great way to start building positive relationships. Some of these relationships might be very important as you are planning for your life after sport. You might even meet your mate or your future business partner. Some student athletes on other teams, especially ones who are isolated because of facility location, may be harder to access. Don't let that be an excuse. There are plenty of opportunities to get to know athletes from other sports in class, study hall, training room, dining hall, etc.

Your Mate

It's important to treat everyone you meet with respect, whether you think they deserve it, or not. I believe the value of respect can take us a long way in relationships. If you choose to have a mate in life, having a strong foundation of respect will be paramount in that relationship. No matter what type of background you come from, you have to establish respect. Respect should be a mutual value between people who want to maintain meaningful relationships. I have coached athletes who understand this well, and I have also coached athletes who didn't have a good concept of what having a respectful relationship was. Make sure that whomever you choose to spend the most time with respects themselves first. Do not spend your time around people who do not respect themselves first because it's almost impossible for them to respect you and others in return. As a coach, I would always tell athletes to respect the person you're interacting with, no matter if you think they deserved it or not. Approaching people this way will never backfire on you. You may not like the responses all the time, but you can always walk away with your integrity and reputation intact. I've seen too many athletes get into trouble because the person they're spending their time with did not respect who they were. I've also coached athletes who didn't understand respect well enough and put themselves in situations that led to unfortunate circumstances.

If the person you are spending your time with isn't a person you feel deserves your respect, then choose to spend your time with someone else. You never know if the person who you are spending a lot of time with will be your lifelong mate. This decision will be one of the most important decisions you'll ever make. It is important to make sure this person is the right person for you. You want to make sure that you are spending your time with someone in a positive relationship that helps you to be a better person just like you are helping them to be a better person.

Coaches, Teachers, and Professors

In my experience, too many athletes view their coaches as only coaches, their teachers as only teachers, and their professors as only professors. Too many athletes never look past what those people do professionally to see the human being side. Developing relationships with your coaches, teachers, and professors can be some of the most valuable relationships you've ever invested in. Let me give you an example. I remember getting cut from the San Diego Chargers and calling a former coach and professor. Both were very helpful to me in a time of need. Can you imagine having a positive relationship with a college professor and being able to call them for help after you get cut from a team while being a professional athlete? Who do you think can help you more than the people who spend most of their time trying to help you? As a coach, I've written countless letters of recommendations for former athletes. I've also hired several of our student athletes to work on our staff. How I got started in the strength and conditioning profession is because my college strength and conditioning coaches extended an opportunity to me to work with them on their staff. I was actually offered a graduate assistantship while I was a professional athlete. I had developed such a strong relationship with my college strength and conditioning coaches that my wife and I asked one of my strength coaches and his wife to be the God-parents to our children. Once again, the point here is make sure you are investing in positive relationships with people who are trying to help you. These people will be some of the best resources you'll ever have.

Academic Staff and Other Support Staff

If you are a college student athlete or if you have ever been a college student athlete, then you know you spend most of your time not with your sport coaches, but with the support staff. The support staff includes the academic staff, nutrition staff, sports medicine staff, sports performance staff, counselors, advisors, etc. Many athletes take advantage of these people and build positive relationships. These people can be your biggest advocates for your current and future opportunities. It's important to be mature enough to view these people as not there to give you something, but as great resources.

If you know who you are and what you want to be, it'll be much easier to understand how to best utilize these people and the resources they provide. Student athletes who hadn't connected their purpose and passion to what they were doing, academically, and for career preparation, often struggle with the proper motivation to be productive. The athletes who know or have an idea about what they want to do are highly motivated and tend to better utilize resources such as study hall, tutors, mentors, etc. In my experience, I found we didn't have to chase academically motivated student athletes around campus to get them to take care of their business.

Why do so many student athletes leave many academic opportunities and resources on the table? When I speak to high school student athletes, I ask them about advanced placement (AP), honors classes, and other opportunities to achieve college credit. Many of them haven't taken advantage and some don't know enough about the opportunities to do so. You should at least explore how you can enter college with college credits. This route may not be as difficult as you think to be able to take advantage of this. I recently had the opportunity to coach Blaise Taylor. Blaise graduated with a Bachelor and MBA degree in only three and a half years. He entered college with college credits from high school and he took a full course load in college. When I look at Blaise and I think back to my own academic path, I am reminded how much I left on the table. I wasted several opportunities. The fact is, I didn't know any better. Not just me, but several opportunities were lost with many of my teammates as well. I believe only one of my college teammates graduated in four years who was in the same incoming recruiting class. The rest of incoming class, including me, took five years or longer to graduate, or never graduated at all. I remember being confused how the one who graduated in four years could've done that. The answer is clear—he had the knowledge and the motivation to do so. The rest of us were not fully utilizing the resources and opportunities that were right in front of us. Most of us didn't enter college with any college credits and we took the minimum amount of credit hours each semester in college. Most of my incoming class believed we were going to the NFL. We didn't spend much time talking about what we were going to do after we were done playing football.

Academic resources today have improved dramatically over the past twenty years. There is no excuse for any student athlete to not be able to choose the career path they want to pursue and be successful in life. The resources available today academically and counseling-wise are much more expansive. Make sure you are developing positive relationships with the academic and support staff as you spend most of your time with these people in college.

Principals, Athletic Directors, and Campus Administrators

Believe it or not, most of your principals, athletic directors, and campus administrators want to see you succeed. It's important to build positive relationships with these people, too. They are very influential and their networks are vast. If you need a part-time job, internship, or recommendation for a full-time job, these are the people that you want to make sure you engage. If you're a student athlete in high school, your campus leaders can help you get to college. Or, if you are a student athlete in college, they can help you with your career path. Most of the principals, athletic directors, and campus administrators, I have met, are very proud of the student athletes they represent. Many are connected with the community, and many businesses, locally, regionally, and nationally. They have many relationships with many business people who are always looking to hire former student athletes.

Businesses, Donors, and Alumni

Some of the biggest supporters of an athletics program are business owners, donors, and alumni. When I was a student athlete, I was always told to stay away from boosters. The reason is that some of these supporters have crossed the lines in the past by providing impermissible benefits. As student athletes, we were never taught how to interact with our biggest supporters. There are many occasions where student athletes come in contact with the very people that can help them the most in life after sport. I have attended events where donors are in the same room as the student athletes. Much later, after my collegiate athletic career was over, I realized how I used to let these opportunities pass by due to the lack of knowledge and awareness. Fortunately, I went into coaching back at my Alma Mater after my playing career was over. I was able to capitalize on many of the relationships I left on the table as a student athlete.

My advice to current student athletes is to take advantage of the opportunities to establish a proper relationship with business owners, businesses, donors, and alumni. When you attend an event, introduce yourself and find out about what these valuable people do professionally. Exchange contact information and reach out occasionally to build and maintain your professional network. There is nothing illegal about establishing a professional relationship. Just make sure that you do not accept any impermissible benefits or cross any line of demarcation as a current student athlete. Maybe you can secure an internship while you are a current student athlete in the field that you want to pursue. Maybe there is a chance you can work at the company affiliated with the person you met at the athletic event. The experience and information you could potentially capture due to the fact you are a student athlete is hard to place a value on. As a student athlete you have a certain amount of fame and while there are rules (for now) limiting you from actualizing or cashing in on how people see you, you can still make the most of the opportunities without committing a violation.

Banks

I have played and coached in many stadiums and arenas with names of major national banks on the signage of the building. Seeing this inspired me to have many conversations with student athletes about banks, finances, investments, money, and wealth. Whenever I had these conversations with athletes, they would be very interested in that exchange of information. Some of them were much more knowledgeable than I was at their age about money, finances, and investments. I have also had conversations with athletes in the past who didn't even have a bank account. I would often ask student athletes questions about loans and investment accounts. Some of them would have a good base of information, but most did not. I would ask them how can they play in a stadium or an arena named after a Bank and not know anyone who is associated with that bank. They would tell me, "That's a great question." Some of the conversations would go very deep and sometimes they would ask questions which I did not have answers to. I remember once going to the bank to get some of their questions answered. Many of the athletes I would have conversations with wanted to be entrepreneurs. I would ask them, "If you plan to be an entrepreneur, do you have a relationship with the people who can loan you the money to create your startup?" Ninety-nine percent of the time the answer would be, "No." I would then ask them, "Do you think some of those people come to watch you play?" Their answer would be, "Yes!"

My advice to you as a current student athlete is to approach your coaches and athletic administrators and ask them for assistance with establishing relationships with the people who can help you the most after you're done playing. You need to start establishing those relationships while you are a current student athlete. If you wait until after you graduate, you will have lost time and many opportunities to build these personal and professional relationships. If you are a former student athlete, you can still find ways to capitalize on the fact you were a student athlete. Hopefully you established some good relationships with the people in your athletics department and your coaches while you were a student athlete.

Community Relations, Local Government, and Chamber of Commerce

Community service is a great opportunity to develop relationships with people who live in the same communities where you go to school. Developing relationships with people and leaders in the community is a great way to utilize your platform as a student athlete to help and inspire others. People in the community love when athletes engage and interact with residents in the community. You have a chance to get to know some of your local government officials or members of your Chamber of Commerce. These can be valuable relationships to establish. The people that work in local government and the Chamber of Commerce are powerful, influential, and well-connected in the community. If you can call on these people when it is time for you to transition to your life after sport, you'll have an advantage.

Professional athletes learn that their bodies are their business. This is one of the reasons why I talk to the student athletes as though they are future entrepreneurs. Some educators I've been around call this an asset-based approach. If you can take the values and lessons you have learned as a student athlete and apply them to your professional career goals, you can go further than you thought possible. As a current or former student athlete, you can use your platform to help others.

There is something about sports and athletics that help people come together to aspire to do more. There is nothing more rewarding than giving back to the people in the community that support or supported you as a student athlete. Coaches and administrators often encourage student athlete engagement and community relations for many reasons. One of the most beneficial outcomes of engaging with the community can be the development of the student athlete's character. Coaches know that if they can help to develop the character of their student athletes, it will have a positive correlation with the team's chemistry. Coaches want the team culture to be positive and to have a positive culture you have to have great team chemistry. We can all use sport to help us make our communities better places to live.

Media

The way relationships get portrayed between athletes and the media has always been troublesome to me. The media members I knew when I was a student athlete and coach have been some of the most helpful people to me in my personal and professional life. The idea that most of the media is always out to get athletes is false. Most of the time, the media people I have been associated with are good people and want the best for the athletes they are interacting with. I was able to develop some very good relationships with the media during the time when I was a student athlete. I can call many of these people today if I ever need their assistance, and they know they can call on me.

As a student athlete, make sure you understand the line that should not be crossed when you were dealing with the media. But also understand how these people can help you if you have the right awareness and understanding. The media have also been some of the best promoters to student athletes' private efforts. I have coached athletes who started their own not-for-profit foundations and the media assisted with the promotion. Some media members have even served as board members on athletes' foundations. Don't fall into the narrative that all media is bad. They want to be good at what they do just as much as you want to be good at what you do. If you can have a mature perspective, you can understand how to collaborate with the media so they get what they want, and you get what you want.

I cannot place more emphasis on the importance of building and investing in positive relationships. Networking is all about relationship building. To be successful in life, you cannot do it all by yourself. You need other people to help you along the way. Successful teams or companies have people that are helping each other out all the time. To think and care only about yourself is selfish and counterproductive to progress. I've heard coaches say, "It's not about you, it's only about the team," and I disagree. I believe saying that "it's not about you" creates the absence of accountability. I believe it should be ALL about you getting it done for yourself and for others. I believe it's about you getting your job done and being accountable to your responsibilities and accepting consequences for your own actions. For you to bring the best version of you into your relationships, you need to respect yourself first. Make sure the people you spend the most time with are positive people so you can have positive relationships.

MONEY AND WEALTH

Before you speak, listen. Before you write, think. Before you spend, earn. Before you invest, investigate. Before you criticize, wait. Before you pray, forgive. Before you quit, try. Before you retire, save. Before you die, give.

—William A. Ward

After I had the opportunity to be a collegiate athlete at the University of Missouri, I was able to go on to be a professional athlete in the National Football League. I saw many layers of the economics revolving around sports. As a former student athlete, I can say that few high school and college student athletes are prepared to be professional athletes outside of playing the sport itself. I believe as a coach, it was my responsibility to teach the athletes about how to best prepare themselves to avoid the negative statistics.

Most of the professional athletes I played with didn't know the difference between money and wealth. Very few of the professional athletes I played with owned businesses or had a knowledgeable understanding about investments. I remember as a rookie in the NFL I heard more stories about how to spend money than how to keep or save money. As a matter of fact, I don't remember ever having a conversation about how to start a business or build wealth. Of the hundreds of professional athletes I played with, maybe only a dozen of them had their own businesses outside of football. Probably the most successful professional athlete I played with had his own restaurant and had over $1 million stolen away from him through bad investment relationships. The equivalency of that $1 million in salary today would probably be around $20 million or more!

When I was a rookie, one of the veterans told me a story about how he spent all his money his rookie year. It took him over an hour and a half of storytelling, going into detail about how he spent every dollar, or should I say wasted every dollar. His story was outrageous! He talked about all the money he spent on diamonds, cars, gold chains, parties, women, etc. I still remember many of the details he talked about because I had never heard of anything like that before in my life. He talked about all the money that was garnished from his wages because of child-support. He talked about staying in a hotel and renting the whole property for a draft party. As I look back on that moment and how he lived his life it makes me sad. The worst part of his story is he ended his life by suicide. This was such a waste of life potential. His story is also part of the reason I'm so passionate about educating student athletes.

Since being a student athlete, I've learned that money is not the same as wealth. Money is just a convenient pathway by which we can accumulate wealth. Money is what people talk about 99% of the time. Student athletes are rarely taught about wealth or how to save and keep your money. We promote to recruits how much money former student athletes have made as professional athletes, but there are no statistics about how much of that money is saved or invested. In my understanding, wealth is attained when your money is making money. If you are a student athlete in high school or college, you can start by saving or educating yourself about small investments.

I coached an athlete who once told me he regretted some of the decisions he made about how he spent his money. He had decided to go out and buy a brand-new Dodge Charger and put on a new set of aftermarket rims and tires. He told me he didn't realize how much he would have to spend on insurance, maintenance, and gas. He was in debt as a college student athlete while on full scholarship. I coached other athletes who have fetishes for expensive material items such as gym shoes. One athlete I coached would buy a new pair every month. I remember having a conversation with him about spending money. He told me that purchasing these shoes was an investment and sometimes he could resell them used for more than he bought them. I didn't agree, but I accepted his argument as a good stance because at least he was thinking about his purchases with a business mind-set.

I'm not an expert on financial matters, money, or wealth so I asked for help from Dr. Starla Ivey. She's a personal finance professor and also my wife. When we met in college she was working at a bank. She has dedicated over twenty years of her life to helping people, especially students and athletes, become more financially literate. Many of her students have told her the class they took with her was their favorite and most important class they took in college. Dr. Ivey has also taught personal finance in China as a guest professor at Chongqing University of Technology. It is amazing to me that personal finance is not a class taught in every high school and university. I hope you read this chapter and have a better understanding of personal finance and how to apply it.

The second person I asked to write on the subject of money and wealth is Coach Derek Lege. Coach Lege is the Head Strength and Conditioning Coach at the University of Texas-Tyler. Coach Lege was on staff with us at the University of Missouri and served as a graduate assistant. He has since gone on to be a full-time assistant and now is a full-time Director of Strength and Conditioning and Athletic Performance. Coach Lege spent his free time learning about stocks and investing in the stock market. He is not a Certified Financial Planner, but he does have some knowledge that you, as a student athlete, can apply. Hopefully, you can begin to understand some investment concepts before you make it as a professional. Maybe before you start your career, you can start on a smaller level and once you start earning income from your job, you'll be able to do more.

PERSONAL FINANCE
(BY DR. STARLA IVEY)

Although many high school students would like to learn more about personal finance, very few have had this opportunity before coming to college. In fact, most college students haven't been exposed to a personal finance class even after graduating from a postsecondary institution. Understanding even the basics of money management can help with your financial fortitude that impacts your personal well-being while in school and after graduation. One of the financial pitfalls that students succumb to is taking on large amounts of student loan debt relative to the amount they can payoff. The ramifications of this can result in making payments for decades and many find themselves postponing life events such as moving out of their parents' home, completing dental procedures, having children, and even foregoing marriage. In fact, research states that college-age students are ill-equipped to handle their own finances and don't understand how their decisions today impact their financial future. The need for financial education is evident with the number of adults citing financial issues as the cause of their personal anxiety/stress and marital discourse.

With all the advanced technology and manpower vested to enhance a student athlete's athletic and academic performance, it makes sense to develop their financial well-being also. Some athletic programs have been forward thinking and have offered financial literacy to their athletes in the form of guest speakers, workshops, and even classes dedicated to managing finances to prepare them for life after sport. Some student athletes find themselves in the unique situation of going professional in their sport. With immediate five to six figure leaps in income, personal finance basics such as budgeting, saving, investing, and paying off debt is a must—learning these principles early on allows the student athlete to make better financial decisions in a fast-paced, complex environment. Despite astonishingly high incomes, professional athletes file for bankruptcy at an alarmingly high rate relative to the average American.

While in college, a student athlete has a very occupied day, from early morning workouts, class, and practice to dinner and study hall (early to bed and early to rise to start all over again the next day). Whether you've earned a scholarship or are financing through student loans with such a demanding schedule and rules governing outside employment, budgeting and money management are a key for your limited income possibilities. For many student athletes, this may be their first time handling their own money choices and may be more money than they have dealt with in their entire life thus far. Many may think their scholarship will cover all their expenses while in college, but this is probably not the case. What do you do with any funds left over once tuition and fees are paid? Where will you live (on campus or off campus)? Where can you eat and how much does it cost vs having a meal plan on campus? Will you have any money left over after the necessities of school, food, and housing? Will your scholarship be enough to cover the costs of education and if not, how do you finance the rest of my college career? It doesn't matter if the student athlete will sign a $1.5 million contract or they graduate 5-6 figures in debt, all student athletes need to know about personal finance and how to keep themselves financially sound while in college to put them in a great financial position when they graduate. Financial success starts early to lay the foundation for success later in life.

Creating a budget to estimate income and expenses is an invaluable skill. By doing so, you can estimate how much money you'll have coming to you every month and also the expenses that you'll incur during that time. Living by a budget helps to alleviate some of the stressors of overspending by creating a sense of security that there is enough money to pay bills or identifying shortfalls. Budgeting is not fool-proof. Just like in sports, athletes practice very hard. However, the end result is not always a win—the hope is continual improvement, whether that is in your sport or creating a workable budget.

Budgeting

Budgeting is a very simple process in which you dedicate a certain portion of your income (or money that you have) for a particular expense. For example, after paying rent and school bills, let's say you have $500 remaining for the month; however, you still need to pay utilities for your apartment and food to eat. How will you divide your spending for the month? You may dedicate $250 for food (going out to eat and groceries), $100 for your utilities, and $100 for your car payment (your parents have graciously offered to pay for your gas and insurance). This leaves you with $50 remaining each month. How will you allocate the remaining portion? Will this go into a savings account for an emergency fund? Will this be your fun money that you spend on entertainment?

Some people like to call this the envelope method as you dedicate a portion of your funds to each of your expenses—some people literally divide their money into envelopes and pull out cash when needed. For instance, when you go to the grocery store you take your grocery envelope to pay for your items. But what happens if you run out of money in the grocery envelope before the end of the month and you still need to buy groceries? You could use money from your entertainment envelope or possibly use your utilities fund (hint: you don't want to utilize your utilities fund as your electricity will get cut off). The hope is that at the end of the month all your bills are paid, and all of your envelopes are empty or near empty. It may take several tries before you come up with a combination of dedicated amounts for your bills before you find one that works well for you and your spending habits. Also, you may find that instead of changing the amount that you spend in each category, it may be easier to change your spending habits. Instead of going out to eat every day, you decide to make breakfast and dinner at home and bring a refillable cup for water during the day. You may decide that instead of keeping your thermostat at seventy degrees in the summer, you raise it up to seventy-five degrees in order to save money.

First develop an income and expense statement to estimate (1) how much income you will receive each month and (2) the categories of expenses and how much you will spend in each. Remember that this is just an estimate and that your income and expenses might change depending on the month. For instance, if you celebrate Christmas with gifts, your expenses may be higher in December than in other months or if you are able to work in the summer, your income may be more then than during your sporting season. Below is a sample income and expense statement to help you forecast each category that you are budgeting. This is a great way to prepare for upcoming financial changes in your life - going to college, getting married, having a baby, just to name a few. Your categories may look similar (you can add, and change categories as fits best with your lifestyle and spending habits).

Income and Expense Statement for 2020

	Jan	Feb	Mar	Apr	May	Jun	Jul	Aug	Sep	Oct	Nov	Dec
Income from Job	0	0	0	0	1000	1000	1000	0	0	0	0	0
Scholarship	11k	500	500	500	500	500	500	11k	500	500	500	500
Total Income	11k	500	500	500	500	1.5k	1.5k	11k	500	500	500	500
Rent	300	300	300	300	300	300	300	300	300	300	300	300
Food	100	100	100	100	100	100	100	100	100	100	100	100
Tuition	10.5k	0	0	0	0	0	0	10.5k	0	0	0	0
Utilities	45	40	35	30	30	45	45	40	35	30	30	45
Entertainment	35	35	35	35	35	35	35	35	35	35	35	35
Gifts	0	0	0	0	25	25	0	0	0	0	0	100
Cell Phone	75	75	75	75	75	75	75	75	75	75	75	75
Total Expenses	11,055	550	545	540	565	580	555	11,050	545	540	540	655
Net Income (income minus Expenses)	-55	-50	-45	-40	-65	+920	+945	-50	-45	-40	-40	-155

Although there is a shortfall every month except for June and July, the extra money saved during the summer is more than enough to cover the remaining months. Now think about this—what if you went home during the summer to work, live with your parents, and sublease your apartment. This would allow you to cut a lot of expenses during the summer months and save even more for the school year when expenses may be higher, and you are unable to work due to sport obligations.

Once you feel comfortable with practicing your income and expense statement on paper, put it into practice and create an actual budget. Below is a sample budget representing the estimates that you calculated in the income and expense statement along with the actual expenses that you had for that month. Remember this is a work in progress and every month may not work out perfectly with a zero account, but the hope is to continually improve.

Budget for the month of April 20**

Rent	_Food_	_Tuition_	_Utilities_
$300 estimate	$100 estimate	$0 estimate	$30 estimate
$300 actually spent	$30 groceries	$0 actually spent	$25 actually spent
-----$0 -----	$10 dining out	-----$0 -----	-----$5 -----
	$35 groceries		
	$15 dining out		
	$30 groceries		
	$25 groceries		
	------$45 -----		
Entertainment	_Gifts_	_Cell Phone_	
$35 estimate	$0 estimate	$75 estimate	
$20 actually spent	$20 actually spent	$70 actually spent	
-----$15 -----	------$20 -----	-----$5 -----	

Nowadays there are several apps that can assist you with budgeting that will also run some basic reports so you can see your exact spending habits each month. Apps such as YNAB (You Need a Budget), Mint, Acorns, Monefy, and Robinhood are geared toward young adults. Some of these are free while others charge a monthly fee. They also vary with the amount of personal finance tools they offer - budgeting, saving, bill pay, tracking expenses, investing, etc. For example, YNAB has a specific feature that will notify when you have overspent in one of your categories and ask you to choose another category to fund the expenses. Mint and Robinhood not only provide budgeting features but also allow you to monitor your investments. Acorns allows you to invest your spare change to assist you in saving effortlessly. Whichever app you choose, remember to keep your budget simple and make it customized for your spending habits.

Saving

You may find it hard to save during college; however, there are ways you can still live fabulously and save some money.

1. If you decide to devote yourself to creating a savings, make sure and pay yourself first. Thus, you do not wait until the end of the month to see how much money you have left, budget your savings first. It will pay off in the end.

2. Live with roommates whether it is in the dorm or in an apartment. Splitting up the bills among two to four people makes it easier than footing the bill yourself.

3. Sweat the small stuff – buying a Starbucks latte or a Coca Cola out of the vending machine adds up when spending $2–$4 dollars a day. Brew your own coffee from home and buy packs of soda at the grocery

(or just drink water—student athletes should stay hydrated).

4. Bring your own lunch—dining out at your favorite fast food restaurant may be convenient but it can be costly at $10–$20 per meal. Maybe start with one day of the week and see how much you can save by making your own meals—who knows it could be a lot of fun and a good way to impress your friends with your culinary skills.

5. Old Phrase—don't try to keep up with the Jones or the Kardashians: Sure it would look great for an Instagram photo to impress your friends but how much does that new outfit really cost and can you really afford it? Knock offs are great and second-hand stores are a gem—add a little of the new with the old.

Saving with the power of compound interest: Here's something to ponder on—let's say you have an extra $200 this month that you can spend on anything you want. Maybe you buy a pair of $200 gym shoes or maybe you put the $200 in the stock market. Which one caters to your sense of immediate gratification and which one caters to your future self? Well, let's fast forward twenty-five years from now - if you chose the gym shoes, how much are they worth now (probably nothing); now let's look at the stocks you purchased. Utilizing what's called compound interest, you would have almost $700 in the account. Imagine if you did that each month! The point is to have your money work hard for you, and not you working hard for your money. When you are ready to graduate from college, you could have a professional writer rework your resume—it may cost you $300; however, you may be able to earn up to $5000 more a year on your first job—now that's a great return on your investment.

Being a student athlete is an honor that only few college students get an opportunity to do—have fun, enjoy different experiences, learn lots, and keep improving in life and sport!! Your future self will thank you.

INVESTMENTS
(BY DEREK LEGE)

Why do most people think negatively about money? Some say the rich deceive the poor to get rich or keep getting rich. I believe it is a lack of education—we already know schools don't emphasize financial literacy. Often because of debt and/or financial illiteracy, indicators today are pointing toward people waiting longer to get into the stock market. One area we can agree with is the stock market can help achieve financial goals if done early enough and with patience and the right knowledge. If a college athlete took $10 and saved it every week for four to five years in college, assuming a rate of return of 8%, they would have over $3,000 by the time they graduate. This amount goes up exponentially if they can save more.

The questions I get a lot from college athletes are how much money do I need to start investing? How can I invest as a student athlete who doesn't make much money or has any income? Where do I invest? One of the more important questions asked is, "Isn't investing risky and isn't it possible I can lose all my money?" My answer to that question is yes it CAN be. Putting your money into something you have very little knowledge of or no knowledge at all is gambling or speculation. To begin, I ask athletes, what is investing? Investing is putting your money into something now with the expectation that will be of higher value later. One's goal for putting money to work is to grow it over time in an investing vehicle. One may be advised to hire a financial advisor to handle or control their investments. I encourage young individuals to learn how to invest because no one will take care of your money as you will. Now, the question then becomes what are your goals for investing? What do you want to gain? These questions initiate a series of questions one begins to ask themselves. How much money is acceptable to retire? Is 4% to 6% percent returns enough to grow my account in x amount of years? We all must start somewhere, and like most college athletes, we do not have much money to start. Investing is not a get rich quick scheme. The good news is you can grow your wealth despite not having much money to begin investing. Not having much money in the beginning is good because it makes one do their homework before investing. I am a fan of value investing, which means I would prefer to buy something worth $10 for only $5. Value investing is how the investing mogul Warren Buffett made millions early in his career. Investing with a small account is like investing with a million dollars—the amount changes but the investing principles remain. Small accounts with $1,000 or less should consider purchasing individual stocks of reputable companies. It is not much, but it's a start and one could take more chances with the hope of earning a higher rate of return. Taking calculated risks sounds good, but now you ask yourself, "What is a great company?" Start by asking yourself, "What do I love?" "What do I know?" "Do I understand the business?" I love technology and how it makes most of our lives much more efficient. Technology has made advancements so quickly— smartphones, smart TVs, smart homes, self-driving vehicles, etc. These things require a huge memory capacity. I researched top companies leading the industry in memory, including their fundamentals to find which would give me the best return on investment and how they run their business. Then I looked at their competitive advantage over their competitors, meaning what they have but their competitors don't?

Lastly, is it on sale? What is the company worth, and what is its current value? Will this company's value be worth more in three to five years than it is today? If yes, then I make the purchase. If not, maybe it goes on my watch list and I move on. If I purchase a share of a business, I am looking for returns of 15% or more per year. Remember, it's not the amount that counts, it's the strategy. With the right approach and taking calculated risks, one can quickly grow their money. All this sounds exciting, but how do we come up with $500 or more? One has many responsibilities when living the college life - bills, auto repairs, food, etc. I always tell my athletes that at any time they have income, or a paycheck, they should PAY THEMSELVES FIRST. Paying yourself first is the number one principle for the wealthy. You do not work to pay others first!

Pay at least 10% to 15% to yourself. One can put money paid to themselves in a money market account or just a savings account until one reaches one's goal. In the meantime, this is an opportunity to research or follow a stock that piques your interest. There are resources out there that allow you to virtual trade, or in the old days - they call it paper trading. Paper trading or virtual trading means you use fake money to try out a strategy or test a theory about purchasing a stock. This way if you make a mistake, it doesn't cost you anything. Another benefit to not having money to start investing is forming saving habits. Saving money is a learnable skill. One cannot say once they have x amount of dollars, they will set aside y amount to save. It doesn't work that way. Here is a perspective. Can you fathom keeping $10 for every $100 you earn? How about saving $10,000 from $100,000? Same principle but a different amount. When you haven't had this kind of money, it is hard to think you can set aside $10,000. Saving every little bit of money can help tackle this mental block. Remember this: poor people spend first, save later. Rich people save first and spend what is left.

One might ask how long does investing take? It's natural to want to know how quickly you can make money. There are traders who market day trading to earn income daily. Investing and making money on a daily do not go hand in hand. If that's your goal, gambling or placing a bet on sports is a better choice. Attempting to make money fast is not investing, it is gambling. It takes due diligence which will pay off in the long run. Even though the market is cyclical, it wasn't created to go down. It is a way for companies to raise money to grow. Therefore, if you choose a great company and sit on your hands, it may pay off handsomely.

Once you've decided what type of investor you are and research has been done on a business you love, we then come to the next step of choosing how to go about executing trades. There are many ways to do this from online brokers to robo advisors. Athletes, for the most part, do not have an employer; therefore, investing through their job would not be an option during college. Next, funding an account differs based upon which investing platform you choose. Most do not require a minimum while some will require a minimum deposit. The platform will tell you how to fill out an application; many can even be done online. From there, it's recommended to connect your bank with this new account.

So, what makes the stock market go up or down. Some say news drives direction; it's human sentiment. People's reactions to news dictate the direction a stock goes. If there is news that comes out and the majority tends to have a negative or positive outlook, the market will follow that emotion.

The stock market can be used as a vehicle to achieve your financial goals, whether it is helping family, starting a business, paying toward debt, or financial freedom. With the increasing amount of debt people are facing, living paycheck to paycheck, and the cost of living, young people can help curve this notion by building savings habits as well as getting involved with investing and budgeting. Having too much debt is a threat to one's financial goals. They can charge whatever interest necessary and you must pay. With financial education, young people can create their wealth while encouraging others, such as family, to learn how to save and budget, where to keep money, and everything about investing.

LIVING LIFE

"You only live once, but if you do it right, once is enough."

—Joe Lewis

The final theme in this book is Living Life. The final three chapters discuss Life after sports, focus and family, and passing the baton to teaching others. There are so many opportunities to grow as a person and many experiences that can push you to the maximum limits. This can be very intoxicating and addicting. The bright lights, the fans and cheers from the crowd, the adrenaline rushes, Wow! These are just a few of the exciting experiences you can have as a student athlete. Being a high school and college student athlete can be very rewarding and exciting. On many high school and college campuses, people treat student athletes as though they are celebrities, and on some campuses, they ARE celebrities. Being a student athlete can increase your popularity, notoriety, and accessibility. These experiences can influence who you and others think you are. When so many people around you praise you for your athletic prowess and accolades, it's not easy to remain unaffected. As a student athlete it's easy to hope, think, and believe you will go on to be a professional athlete one day. The quest for being a professional athlete can consume every thought of every minute of the day. In some cases, to be an elite professional athlete those thoughts might consume most of time and energy.

According to an article in the Bleacher Report, the average career in the NFL is reported to be three and a half years. The average career for other professional sports are slightly higher up to five and a half years.

As a coach, I used to ask athletes to do the math of how old they would be after their professional athletic career. Most athletes enter the professional ranks between the ages of twenty and twenty-two. If you add the average professional career to the age most athletes enter, they would be retired between the ages of twenty-five and twenty-seven. The next question I would ask them is, "What are you going to do for the next forty to fifty years of your life?" The answer to that question would usually be the same. That answer would be they weren't sure.

You have to have a purpose and a vision for who you are outside of the sport you are playing. Hopefully you know the answer to the question "What is it you want to do after having a career as a student athlete or a professional athlete?" Knowing the answer to that question can impact what you do while you were playing your sport. You have to prepare yourself for when you are no longer playing your sport. Knowing what you want to do and how you want to have an impact can affect the path you take, academically and socially. As an athlete you have to take some time to think about the day you will no longer be playing your sport.

The greatest chance for success is to be prepared in advance. If you know you love the sport you play so much and it is hard to imagine not being around your sport, then make plans to continue to be around the sport you love. There are many opportunities to work in a high school, a college athletics department, or a professional sport organization. Let me give you an example from my personal life. I knew that I loved sports and being around athletics and I wanted to spend the rest of my life doing that. This is why I became a Strength and Conditioning Coach.

Allow me to share another life lesson I learned from a former Denver Bronco teammate. Let me first share some context for this great advice I received. After getting released from the Broncos, I went back to the University of Missouri and became a graduate assistant in the weight room. Later that year, I had a chance to go back and watch the Broncos play over Thanksgiving week. While I was back in Denver, I stopped by the practice facility and hung out with some of the players in the locker room. David Diaz-Infante, one of the starting of offensive linemen, asked me what I was doing and I told him that I was a graduate assistant Strength and Conditioning Coach. He asked me if I was done playing professionally and I told him I still had dreams. He told me it was ok to continue to pursue my dream as long as I was making progress in life outside of being an athlete. That would be one of the most important conversations I've ever had and his advice provided the direction I needed as I was preparing to make my transition from being an athlete to a coach.

During the time I was a professional athlete, I also went to graduate school and worked in the weight room. I was a graduate assistant Strength and Conditioning Coach at the University of Missouri while I was also with the Green Bay Packers. I spent six months during the off-season and preseason training and preparing to make the team. While I was in Green Bay, I developed a very good relationship with the strength and conditioning and sports medicine staff. They knew about my goals and aspirations to be a Strength and Conditioning Coach. Well, let me tell you what happened. I ended up playing my last preseason game on a Monday night versus my former team, the Denver Broncos. I was released the next day and headed back to Missouri to re-establish myself as an assistant in the weight room. Shortly thereafter, I received another call from the Green Bay Packers. This time they were offering me a newly created position as Strength and Rehabilitation Coach where I would help out in the weight room and the training room. I was then faced with a difficult decision. Do I continue my path toward receiving my masters' degree as a graduate assistant at the University of Missouri or go to work for the Green Bay Packers? You might be surprised, but I chose to stay at the University of Missouri and continue my career as a Strength and Conditioning Coach. Even though I chose to keep coaching in college, until this day, I still have maintained my relationship with strength coaches, Barry Rubin and Mark Lavatt. I went back and completed my incomplete classes and finished grad school the next year.

That was a long time ago, but it seems like it was just yesterday. Today, I have been married to the person I met in college and we have two beautiful daughters. I have spent over twenty years coaching and climbed the mountain to be recognized as one of the best. I also recognize, I have never done anything by myself. It has always been about the people I have been around. Together, we were able to be great role models for the athletes we coached. We were able to show them there was life after sports and what happens when you focus on family. Together, we were able to pass the baton to thousands of student athletes. If you are a current student athlete and you have good coaches who also happen to be good people, make sure you take the time to tell them "thank you."

LIFE AFTER SPORTS

The proudest moments I had as a Collegiate Strength and Conditioning and Athletic Performance Coach was not the many championships, bowl games, or victories. But, in fact, the proudest moments for me personally were the moments when former athletes returned to campus having been successful in life after sports. If we were in the weight room, I would pause the entire weight room session to have the former player speak to the team. These opportunities were special and I always felt the need to capture the moment. A similar message from a former athlete to current athletes always resonated differently than the same message coming from a coach.

I can think of many other awesome testimonies of former players. A particular proud moment for me was when a former player came back with his spouse and son and they both addressed the lifting group as a couple. This was a really powerful moment. All of a sudden, some of the players in the room saw the reality of the decisions and choices they were making.

They saw the power in having positive relationships. That former player was an entrepreneur, husband, father, and a former stand-out collegiate football student athlete.

Many athletes struggle once they have completed their athletic eligibility because they don't have a plan. The old saying goes "failing to plan is planning to fail." Not having a plan can lead to all sorts of situations that could have been avoided or controlled. Many of the former teammates and athletes I have coached had to face a serious reality once the bright lights of being an athlete turned off in the stadium or arena. They found themselves faced with the questions, "Who am I without my sport? Who am I if I am no longer the student athlete or the professional athlete? Who am I when I no longer am running out of the tunnel?" There is a stark reality that one day you will experience your last play, match, game, etc. What have you done to prepare for that moment? Do you have a plan in place that is ready to activate? Have you prepared yourself emotionally for when the bright lights go out?

Another aspect often overlooked is you also have to make sure you are physically ready for your transition. Some athletes go to some extreme measures to train their bodies to play the sport which they were committed. Some of these measures and behaviors may have positive effects on your longevity, while others may have a negative effect. Many athletes were used to training up to four hours a day when they were competing. Some were used to consuming huge amounts of calories to offset the energy they were expending. Physically, there are many positives to take into life once you're done playing your sport. The nutritional knowledge can be very beneficial when applied in life after sport. Personally, I believe you should continue to treat and train yourself as though you were still an athlete once you were done playing. You will have to make some modifications, but much of the knowledge you have can be applied to keep yourself healthy.

To keep yourself healthy, one of the best skills you can learn while you are an athlete is how to cook for yourself. The more you can learn about food preparation while you are an athlete, the better you will be able to take care of yourself later in life. Most athletes today have some sort of training table or dining hall where they eat most of their meals. If you can learn to prepare food in a healthy way now, the better prepared you will be when you no longer have access to the dining hall. Take advantage of the grocery store tours the Nutrition Staff conducts. If all you have learned to do is order fast food or have it delivered, one day you may regret not using all your resources. Learn how to cook foods like rice, chicken, fish, pasta, vegetables, etc. Learn how to cook your own pizza, hamburgers, or healthy French fries. Just like any other skills you learned while being an athlete, cooking is just a skill and you have to practice. This will be even more important as you get older because food can fuel and heal your mind, body, and spirit.

Make sure you continue your annual health checks and screening. As an athlete, you were required to participate in physicals and exams. Once you are no longer on a sports team you will be solely responsible for your own mental and physical health. Some athletes neglect their health and no longer go to the doctor. As an athlete, you may have had access to a doctor or physician every day. There are many health issues you were able to address just because you had access to medical personnel. There also have been some health issues you could not avoid because you were an athlete. You will need to continue to address those health issues and take restorative measures into your own hands. Controlling your body weight will be one of the biggest challenges you will face as a former athlete. The calories consumed and expended do not equal what they used to. Body weight is one of the most important concerns you will face, as you are no longer a competitive athlete. Getting regular health checks, staying physically active, and eating healthy are some of the most important components to living a healthy life after sport.

In sports, we have made tremendous strides with placing emphasis on education and graduating. An area that is under-emphasized is the importance of how you publicly share your social life. In particular, I am talking about social media. Many athletes have taken advantage of their social media platforms to promote themselves in a positive light. Others have made many mistakes which have costed them opportunities in the present and in the future. Many people are very interested to know more about athletes. Athletes gain followers faster than many other people. As an athlete, you have to recognize the power of your influence and learn how you can use this to your advantage. Just as the old saying goes, "There is a flipside to that coin." On the other side is the damage and distraction you can do to your personal and professional life. Some have fallen into the trap of portraying themselves in a negative light. The perception created can be someone who cannot add value to others or organizations. Be careful what you post, like, love, retweet, or repost. Being reckless in this regard can cost you future opportunities, both, personally and professionally. Many athletes have lost their scholarships, sponsorships, and relationships due to thoughtless social media participation. Make sure you use social media with an awareness that it could affect your opportunities and trajectory in life.

I should also point out that even if you have made several mistakes in life you can still rectify those situations. You can always do something positive and get yourself going in the right direction. Even if you earned a degree in a program you're not passionate about, you can still continue your education. If you did not graduate at all, you can still go back to school and get your degree in an area you're passionate about. You may have made decisions that have cost you opportunities, but you can still find ways to recover what you left on the table. It may not be easy or be a lot of fun, but if you really want success, you'll find ways to get it. If you can find opportunities to identify and admit your mistakes, make the corrections, and take action toward a positive direction, you will achieve success. You can always do something to find success. When you ask yourself "What am I leaving on the table as a student athlete or professional athlete?" How do you respond? I'm hoping you will realize the opportunities now and capitalize on what is available.

FOCUS

It's important to have priorities in life because they allow you to set levels of importance on what you value. Priorities allow you to put order to your thoughts and actions. Almost 100% of the very successful athletes I have coached were able to prioritize what was important and not important to them. In this chapter, we are talking about focus because focus is very important. Focus, put simply, is how you think. Focus is where you put your thoughts and where you keep them. The most successful athletes have a tremendous ability to focus on the goals they set. They have a tremendous ability to stay consistent with the process of preparation.

I teach athletes and students focus through the five skills of Dr. Rick McGuire, Dr. Amber Selking, and my project called Building a Culture of Mental Toughness: The Pyramid Model. In this resource we cover these five skills of focus:

1. Positive self-talk

2. Being present through time orientation

3. Composure using optimal arousal

4. Confidence

5. Concentration

Positive Self-Talk

Self-talk is another term for thinking—your thoughts are your self-talk, an ongoing conversation with yourself. In fact, it is the most influential conversation you ever have. That last statement is what makes it crucial to have positive self-talk! If your ongoing conversation with yourself is negative, it is wrong, and it hurts your performance. But they're your thoughts which means you can control them, and you have the power to change them. You can choose positive self-talk and you can choose to think right with positive thoughts to help your performance in all situations.

When we encounter situations, we have thoughts → our thoughts affect our emotions → our emotions affect our physical being → our physical being affects our behaviors → thus, our thoughts affect our behavior. Our thoughts affect how we play and perform. When we meet challenging or difficult situations and we become upset, we must consciously choose positive self-talk and thinking right.

To help with choosing your thoughts, you can have affirmations prepared ahead of time to make it easy to choose positive self-talk. Affirmations are strong, positive statements about yourself, your team, and/or your mission. They should be strong, rational, strategic, motivating, personal and, of course, positive. Remember this is the most influential conversation you have. It is the conversation with yourself and it's a skill. Having familiarized yourself with these affirmations before-hand will set you up for success when you encounter a difficult situation because you'll have a positive thought ready before you allow a negative thought, to enter your mind.

Below is a list of positive affirmations to get you started:

I am great!

I am strong!

I am prepared!

I am tough!

I am ready!

I trust!

I believe!

I am focused!

I will deliver!

I will do my job!

I will bring my best focus today!

Start fast, finish strong!

Sixty minutes!

No excuses!

Preparation leads to confidence!

We are together!

We are ready!

We are strong!

We are focused!

We will stop them!

We will score!

Positive, affirming, focused thoughts produce the opportunity for consistently great plays for peak performance. Positive self-talk is a skill that can be controlled and is a choice. Positive self-talk is thinking right.

Time Orientation

Focus is a thought which means it's a skill that's completely under your control, you can choose to focus. In choosing to focus, you allow yourself proper time orientation. This is also known as being in the present. This creates the ability to refocus in time for what's next. The past is a time for evaluation where we learn from great performances, mistakes, and from others. The future is a time for planning, goal setting, game planning, and practice. The present is where the magic happens and choosing to focus allows us to be present in our present. "The past is history, the future is a mystery, but today is a gift, that's why they call it a present." Be present in your present. Think Right. You should ask yourself, "Where am I?"

The answer should be, "Right here, right now!" *From Dr. Rick McGuire, "Whistle to the Snap," Time Orientation (Reardon).*

Composure

To be able to perform your best, you must get your arousal to the right level for you. You can be under or over aroused and you will be unable to perform your best. To perform your best, you must find your optimal arousal; find your zone. Luckily for all of us, finding our arousal level is well within our control—it's a choice. We can learn to dial it in perfectly every time by developing the skill using three controls: thought control, breath control, and physical activity control. Thought control is controlling your self-talk and choosing the right thoughts, specifically by choosing arousing affirmations that take you up or relaxing affirmations that bring you down depending on your need for each. Physical activity control is performing active and explosive actions to bring you up or passive and slow actions to bring you down. Lastly, breath control can have huge impacts—a cleansing breath followed by deep abdominal breathing is how you begin breath control. By choosing to emphasize the exhale you will relax and calm down; or you can choose to emphasize the inhale which will energize and excite and bring you up. By choosing to use these three means of control you are literally able to choose the quality of your performance!

Concentration

Not only are we continuously bombarded with information in our perceptual world via our senses, we also use those same senses (sight, hearing, touching, tasting, smelling) to seek out or gain information. Some of the information available to us is relevant to what we are doing (it matters), but you may have also guessed most of the information available to us is irrelevant and does not matter.

For an athlete to deliver great performances they must know the right information to look for, be able to find it, and then stay focused on it. Concentration can be ultimately boiled down to just another way of thinking, which makes it a skill, which makes it controllable, and in turn makes it a choice. This is what concentration is about - concentration is thinking right, distraction is thinking wrong; it's your choice.

I want you to incorporate the following Cook's Model of Concentration routine. This routine follows these four steps:

1. OBSERVE—Find the keys that matter

2. STRATEGIZE—What's the play? What's your job?

3. VISUALIZE—See it! Feel it!

4. TRUST—Trust it! Do it!

Observing athletes will see everything, find the things that matter and focus solely on them. Next is reviewing your strategy – what is the play? What are your responsibilities? What is your job? For imagery, think visualizing yourself delivering a great performance and then see it again, but this time so powerfully that you can feel it. Lastly trust you are focused, trust yourself, and now do it.

Just like learning any new skill, at first this concentration routine may feel awkward. After repetition and remaining consistent, persistent, and relentless it will truly become routine. Commit to choosing to concentrate with this routine. Quickly enough you'll feel comfortable, focused, and confident in the "See it!—Feel it!—Trust it!" routine.

Any number of distractions can try to break your concentration—the last play, a teammate breaking down, deception from opponents, or upsetting calls by the officials. However, they are just distractions and being distracted is thinking wrong. Instead, re-focus and think about what matters and use your concentration routine and voila! The distractions are gone. Best part is that it was your choice. So, you have total control, which really turns into the fact that there are no distractions because you choose for them not to exist. Concentrating on the present or the process can assist with focus, concentrating on the future, or the outcome can interfere with great performance.

Confidence

Confidence is a choice and skill just like the four previous skills of focus. Actually, it's two choices. Choice number one is choosing to become more competent, and choice number two is choosing to focus on your performance. As a student athlete, you have to choose to invest in yourself by investing in your performance. You have to spend time increasing your technical, tactical, physical, and psychological capabilities. You have to spend time getting to know your opponent better than your opponent knows you. Through repetition, competence builds confidence.

As mentioned before, the second choice is choosing to focus on your performance. This means you should focus on the process as opposed to focusing on the outcome. Everyone wants to win, but focusing on the outcome takes away from doing the little things along the way that lead to success. The lack of choosing to focus on your performance is thinking wrong. Performance happens before outcomes. Another piece of advice is to not worry about being the best, but focus on delivering your best. Using your positive affirmations will assist you in staying focused on your performance rather than on outcomes.

FAMILY

I have coached and studied some of the most successful athletes in recent times. I have found a common denominator with successful athletes and successful teams: they all know and understand the importance of family and being a family. The most successful coaches know how to create an environment similar to a big loving family. The most successful athletes know how to use their own family situation as motivation. The most successful teams know how to make the locker room a big family room.

For most people, family is very important. Eventually, you may or may not want to start your own family, or you may be asked to take care of your own family members. Within the context of life after sport, at some point your family will be or will continue to be one of the most important aspects of your life. It's important to know that you carry your family's legacy in who you are and in your last name. There are some very important life decisions you will have to make as former athlete. How you serve your family will be one of the most important decisions you make. Not everyone will decide to get married, and have a spouse and children. However, they will probably have a group of people that they would grow very close to. What I have found is my former teammates are the people who I call my closet friends.

As a former athlete, you will always carry the name of your alma mater and the team you played with for the rest of your life. I am still very close to many of my former high school, college, and professional teammates. The one thing that is true about all these relationships is that those who I spent the most time with, I am now the closest with. Some of my former teammates are called uncles by my children and vice versa. I truly consider my best friends as an extended part of my family.

I was fortunate as a coach to be around head and assistant coaches who wanted to create what we call "a family environment." We realize that many of the athletes we coached needed and wanted a home away from home. They wanted a family environment for many reasons. Some came from backgrounds where their family environment was very good, and some came from backgrounds where it was not very good at all. The one thing we all had in common was when we were in the locker room, everyone was a family member. The most successful teams I was a part of had at least this in common; they were all very close and considered one another as family. This comes down to one basic understanding - caring about teammate. was a core value.

I know without a doubt the people who I have coached and been a teammate of, I can call today and ask for help with just about anything. Once I became a coach it became more evident just how valuable those relationships were. I had a chance to see it from a different perspective as I was trying to help create a great team and family environment. My advice to you as an athlete is, make sure you take every opportunity to take advantage and build those relationships because those people will be a part of you for the rest of your life. They will be your family!

PASS THE BATON TO TEACH OTHERS

"Instruct the wise and they will be wiser still; teach the righteous and they will add to their learning."

—Proverbs 9:9

I have always been very passionate about helping others. Most of the coaches I've been around were in it for the right reasons. The best coaches I had as an athlete were some of the best teachers. As a coach, I always believed in the saying, "you can't coach what you don't teach." Working in athletics has been the most rewarding profession I have ever been a part of. Coaching gave me the opportunity to teach the lessons I learned in life and lessons I wish I knew when I was a student athlete. Some friends of mine encouraged me to write this book because of my passion to educate athletes on knowing the game outside of the game. I personally left many opportunities on the table as an athlete. Since then, I have been working on going back to the table to capitalize on those opportunities. The purpose of this book to get student and professional athletes to be more aware and think more critically about their current situations and opportunities.

The highest level of leadership I achieved as a coach was developing leaders who developed other leaders. This was the best way for me to pass the baton. If you as an athlete have the ability and knowledge to help others, please do. This is how we make our society a better place to live. In my opinion this is the ultimate purpose of our service. If we can help people to help others, we will all be better off.

CONCLUSION

My purpose in life is to help people maximize their human potential. I feel I have been anointed to be a coach and to help young people be the best versions of themselves every day. As a former athlete and young coach, I made many mistakes. I did things I wish I had done better. I spent every day as a coach trying to pass on that knowledge and experience so that the next generation would be better. I hope that as you read this book you can say, "I now have some additional knowledge that will help me over the next few years and for the rest of my life."

The four themes in this book are Choices, Character Development, Money and Wealth, and Living Life. By no means is this book intended to be exhaustive of everything you need to know to be successful. The intention was to bring awareness to some of the recurring themes from my own experiences as a former athlete and coach. You may have other opportunities and choices available to you that are unique. My hope for you is now you can better recognize and capitalize on those moments.

I hope you know what your passion and purpose is so you can be the most motivated person you can be. Don't compare yourself to others and don't worry about being the best, but rather focus on being the best version of yourself every day. There is a game being played every day, whether you are competing or not. If you don't know the game, you are going to get played. Spend time learning about money and wealth on your own. These subjects are rarely taught in school so you will have to do your own research. Finally, I want you to live your life the way you want to the fullest. I don't have many regrets and it feels good to know that for the most part, I made the right decisions with the information I had. My wish for you is to be able to look back and say, "I didn't leave many opportunities on 'The Table,' and when I did, I went back and got what was mine!"

SOCIAL MEDIA

Email: performance@pativey.com
Twitter: @DrCoach_PatIvey
Instagram: @DrCoach_PatIvey
Website: www.PatIvey.com
Facebook: PatIveyPerformance

To listen to my Podcast, *Beyond Sets and Reps*, please go
to: https://beyondsetsandreps.podbean.com

For the video *Building a Culture of Mental Toughness-
The Pyramid Model* is available for purchase at:
https://www.championshipproductions.com/cgi-bin/
champ/p/Performance-Training/Building-a-Culture-
of-Mental-Toughness-The-Pyramid-Model_GD-05436.
html?crm=a-2766

My book *Complete Conditioning for Football* is available for
purchase at https://us.humankinetics.com/products/
complete-conditioning-for-football

ACKNOWLEDGMENTS

I want to say thank you to the Prayer line Warriors. Without your inspiration, this project would not have been completed. Thank you for your accountability, prayers, and encouragement. Special thanks to Dr. Ty Douglas for the connection.

I also want to say thank you to all the Athletic Performance and Sport Coaches who I worked with over the years. Special shout out to the Strength Staff Mafia. I have been very blessed to have worked with you as we poured into thousands of young men and women every day.

RESOURCES

Deci, E. L., & Ryan, R. M. (Eds.). (2004). *Handbook of self-determination research*. University Rochester Press.

Dweck, C. S. (2008). *Mindset: The new psychology of success*. New York, NY: Ballantine Books.

Ivey, P. A. (2013). *Exploring the lived psychosocial experiences of Elite National Football (NFL) players*. Columbia, Missouri: The University of Missouri.

Ivey, P. A., Stoner, J. D. (2012). *Complete conditioning for football*. Champaign, IL: Human Kinetics.

Maxwell, J. C. (2001). *The 17 indisputable laws of teamwork: Embrace them and empower your team*. Nashville: T. Nelson.

Maxwell, J. C. (2011). *The 5 levels of leadership: Proven steps to maximize your potential*. Center Street.

McGuire, R. T. (2012). *From the whistle to the snap: Winning the mental game of football.* Ames, Iowa: Championship Productions.

McGuire, R. T., Ivey, P. A., & Selking, A. R. (2018). *Building a culture of mental toughness: The pyramid model.* Ames, Iowa: Championship Productions.

Warren, R. D. (2002). *The Purpose-driven Life: What on earth am I here for?* Grand Rapids, Michigan: Zondervan.

O'Neill, J. (2000). SMART goals, SMART schools. *Educational Leadership, 57*(5), 46–50.

AUTHORS

Dr. (Coach) Pat Ivey

Dr. (Coach) Pat Ivey is currently the Assistant VP/Associate Athletics Director for Student Athlete Health and Performance at the University of Louisville. He oversees the departments of Sports Medicine, Sports Performance, Sports Nutrition, Mental Health and Performance, and Sports Science. Dr. Ivey is also currently an Adjunct Professor at the University of Missouri, teaching a course in Foundations of Sport Performance via an online Masters' program in Positive Coaching.

Dr. Ivey has also served at the University of Missouri as the Assistant Vice Chancellor for Access and Leadership Development. In this role, he assisted with Community Engagement, Legislative Relations, and K-12 pipelining and programming.

Pat Ivey lettered as a defensive end at Missouri from 1993 to 1995. In 1995, he was honored as being the strongest athlete in the history of Missouri. In 1996, he was signed as a free agent by the San Diego Chargers. Beginning in 1998, Ivey worked as a Graduate Assistant Strength and Conditioning Coach, at the University of Missouri. He started his graduate assistantship after spending time with the Denver Broncos and during his time with the Green Bay Packers in 1999.

His wife, Dr. Starla Ivey, is a college professor and they have two daughters, Paisli and Serena.

Dr. Starla Ivey

Dr. Starla Ivey is a Professor and worked as an Assistant Teaching Professor in the Personal Financial Planning Department at the University of Missouri (Mizzou) for over thirteen years. She taught the Personal and Family Finance course in the undergraduate program and handled under-graduate curriculum. She has also taught for Oklahoma State University. She has both her BS and MS in Personal Financial Planning (Consumer and Family Economics) and a PhD in Human Resource Education, all from the University of Missouri. Before working as an assistant teaching professor, she worked several years as an educational technology special-ist and a recruitment and retention specialist at the collegiate level. She has also worked for State Farm Mutual Insurance, Shelter Insurance, the State of Missouri—Department of Corrections—Accounting Department, and also the Missouri Division of Highway Safety. She is married to Patrick Ivey who holds a PhD in Sports Psychology and they have two daughters, Paisli and Serena.

Derek Legé, Jr.

Derek Legé, Jr. is a Certified Strength and Conditioning Specialist through the National Strength and Conditioning Association. He is a graduate from Ball High School in Galveston, Texas. He earned his bachelor's degree at Texas Southern University in Health Science. He continued his passion for strength and conditioning at the University of Missouri as a graduate assistant while obtaining a master's degree in Education in Counseling, Education, and Sport Psychology.

Coach Legé spent four years at the New Mexico State University as an Assistant Director of Sports Performance and the Director of Nutrition and Student Life Wellness. He currently stands as the Director of Athletic Performance at the University of Texas at Tyler. The past ten years, his interest has continued to grow in personal development, finance, investing, and money management.

He is happily married to Angel Legé for five years and has four children—Torri (eleven), Derek (nine), Amyah (eight), and Amiah (eight).

Akeem Robinson

Akeem Robinson is the Head of Strength and Conditioning at Southeastern University in Lakeland, Florida, and has been a Director of Olympic Sports with ten year of experience rang- ing from NAIA level to Division I. Coach Robinson earned his masters from the University of Missouri in Positive coaching in Psychology, where he worked as a graduate assistant, working with football, cross country, and track and field performance training. Additionally, he helped with social responsibility ini- tiative, "Men for Men," and was the Fellowship of Christian Athletes liaison for the strength staff. During his undergrad, Robinson was a four-year letter winner at Clemson University, and played in four bowl games.